Simple Retreats
for a
Woman's Soul

SUE AUGUSTINE

HARVEST HOUSE™ PUBLISHERS

EUGENE, OREGON

Cover by Left Coast Design, Portland, Oregon

Cover photo © Ligia Botero / Taxi / Getty Images

SIMPLE RETREATS FOR A WOMAN'S SOUL
Copyright © 2001 by Sue Augustine
Published by Harvest House Publishers
Eugene, Oregon 97402
www.harvesthousepublishers.com

Library of Congress Cataloging-in-Publication Data

Augustine, Sue.
  [5-minute retreats for women]
  Simple retreats for a woman's soul / Sue Augustine.
    p. cm.
  Previously published under title: 5-minute retreats for women.
  ISBN-13: 978-0-7369-2307-1
  ISBN-10: 0-7369-2307-1
  1. Women—Psychology—Miscellanea. 2. Women—Conduct of life—Miscellanea 3. Self-help techniques. 4. Relaxation. 5. Pleasure. I. Title.
  HQ1206.A866 2008
  646.70082—dc22

                                                                2007029288

Printed in the United States of America

  08   09   10   11   12   13   14   15   16   / BP-CF /   10   9   8   7   6   5   4   3   2   1

CONTENTS

Innocent Pleasures

7

PART 1

PERSONAL PLEASURES

Innocent Ways to Nurture Yourself

9

Breakfast in Bed ⌒ Start Your Day Refreshed
⌒ Restorative Bathing Rituals ⌒ The
Morning Shower—Alive, Awake, and Alert! ⌒
Hide Out for a Day ⌒ Try Your Hand at
Creativity ⌒ Come Aside and Rest a While ⌒
Enjoy Massage Pleasures ⌒ Give Yourself a
Massage ⌒ Lighten Up ⌒ Play More ⌒
Sweet Dreams

PART 2

COME TO YOUR SENSES

35

Savor the Silence ⌒ The Joy of Listening ⌒
The Sounds of Music ⌒ Create a Nourishing
Tape ⌒ Delight in the Miracle of Touch ⌒
Show Caring Through Touch ⌒ The Pampering
Bath ⌒ Soothing Scents ⌒ The Scent of
a Memory ⌒ Ah, Food, Glorious Food ⌒
A Celebration of Tea ⌒ Tea for One ⌒
Marvel at the Heavens

PART 3

NAME YOUR DAYS

63

Name Your Days ⌒ Laugh a Lot ⌒ Have a
Laugh at Yourself ⌒ Cry a Little ⌒ Groan for
Your Health ⌒ Cultivate a Grateful Heart ⌒
Count Your Blessings ⌒ Give Yourself Away
⌒ Dream a Little Dream ⌒ Find Serenity in
Nature ⌒ Take Time to Meditate

PART 4

INNOCENT ESCAPES

87

Create a Place of Your Own ⌒ Create Your Own
Toy Room ⌒ Visit Your Inner Shangri-la ⌒
Arrange a Minivacation ⌒ Welcome
Unexpected Vacations ⌒ Plan an Imaginary Trip
⌒ Indulge in a Midday Snooze ⌒ Delight in
God's Creatures ⌒ The Inspiring Garden ⌒
Create Your Garden Sanctuary ⌒ A Garden
Anywhere ⌒ The Refreshing Garden ⌒
Rest in a Rocking Chair

PART 5

INSTANT PLEASURES

115

Welcome the Wind in Your Hair ⌒ Go Barefoot
⌒ Find Wonder in Little Things ⌒ Water on
the Inside ⌒ Take a Stroll ⌒ Abandon

Modern Technology for a Day ⌒ Wherever You Are, Be There ⌒ Take Time to Reminisce ⌒ Add a Little Buffoonery to Your Life ⌒ Make Your Own Music ⌒ Dance by Yourself! ⌒ Rejoice in the Wonders of Water

PART 6

TURNING THE PAGES

141

Family and Friends in 8 x 10s: Enjoy the Magic of Photographs ⌒ Escape in a Good Book ⌒ Surround Yourself with Books ⌒ Build Your Personal Library ⌒ Lose Yourself in Children's Books ⌒ Give Poetry a Chance! ⌒ Journal Your Thoughts ⌒ Share the Story of a Lifetime ⌒ Alternative Journals ⌒ Leave a Precious Legacy

PART 7

FAMILY PLEASURES

163

Strengthen Family Ties ⌒ Celebrate a Tradition ⌒ Break from Tradition ⌒ Water Fun ⌒ Play Tourist in Your Hometown ⌒ Play for Free ⌒ Have a Fun and Games Night ⌒ Have a Winter Picnic ⌒ Plan a Treasure Hunt ⌒ Start a Collection ⌒ Enjoy Your Collection ⌒ Memory Gifts ⌒ Put Your Memories on Display ⌒ A Photo Memoir Storybook ⌒ Photo Storybook Themes

PART 8

TEA FOR TWO...OR MORE!

195

Deepen the Bonds of Friendship ⌒ Nurture
Your Friendships ⌒ Hospitality Pleasures ⌒
Tea for Two...or More! ⌒ Meals with Friends
⌒ Spontaneous Entertaining ⌒ Creative
Meals ⌒ Send Thank-You Notes ⌒ Phone a
Friend ⌒ Share the Laughter ⌒ Read to
Someone ⌒ Be Creative in Gift Giving! ⌒
Love and Be Loved

Conclusion

223

INNOCENT PLEASURES

*I believe the nicest and sweetest days
are not those on which anything very
splendid or wonderful or exciting happens,
but just those that bring simple little
pleasures, following one another softly,
like pearls slipping off a string.*

LUCY MAUD MONTGOMERY,
Anne of Green Gables

Are your days filled with working through agendas and meeting deadlines, counting fat grams, eating more fiber, keeping up with yard work and car repairs, fighting off the flu, and practicing self-denial? Are you longing for the pure and simple things of life? In the years that I've been speaking and writing about living with more joy and contentment, I've seen a resurgence of desire for innocent pleasures that will revive our spirits and refresh our souls.

These five-minute retreats describe easy-to-implement experiences that enable us to marvel at the wonders of nature, enjoy the serenity of quiet contemplation, and tap the creativity we need to heal the areas of our lives that are out of balance. They introduce us to innocent pleasures that help us get in touch with how we want to live and then give us vibrant energy to do it.

We've come to mistrust anything not associated with hard work and believe that if something feels or tastes good, it can't be appropriate. Because we've not been encouraged to derive pleasure from ordinary experiences, the absence of joy is more prevalent today than ever. It seems we are no longer inspired by life and routinely deprive ourselves of the delight of playful spontaneity.

With 99 innocent pleasures at your fingertips, you can begin to experience the fullness of living without investing a great deal of time or money. When you are taking life far too seriously and need to recapture lost dreams or gain a fresh perspective, innocent pleasures are good for your body, mind, and soul. Besides stopping to smell the flowers, pause to smell clean sheets, old leather, new books, a turkey roasting, and fresh bread baking. Rediscover simple indulgences like frolicking in a pile of autumn leaves, going barefoot, listening to the rain on the roof, taking a midday snooze, and doing jigsaw puzzles.

Innocent pleasures motivate us to be creative thinkers and positive problem solvers. Scientific evidence suggests that pleasurable experiences may prove to be the most significant ingredients in a long, healthy, effective life because they promote the release of endorphins and boost immunity.

This book is my invitation to you to become immersed in simple indulgences. Let them renew your peace, comfort, and satisfaction. Let them enrich your days and lift your spirits.

PART 1

PERSONAL PLEASURES

Innocent Ways to Nurture Yourself

BREAKFAST IN BED

*Pamper yourself into wellness
with little indulgences.*

ordinarily walk by the lake first thing each morning and then start writing, so having breakfast in bed was not high on my priority list. But when I began incorporating innocent pleasures into my life, I couldn't think of a more appealing way to start the day. So, bright and early one Saturday morning, I meandered into the kitchen and put the kettle on to boil for my favorite English breakfast tea. Then I set up a tray, complete with lace doily and linen napkin, fancy china cup and saucer, the prettiest teapot in my collection, and a few fresh flowers. I blended fresh raspberries with french vanilla yogurt and poured it into a crystal dessert dish. A pineapple-pecan muffin topped it all off.

Once the tea began to steep, the tray, the cat, and I went back upstairs to bed, along with a stack of my favorite gardening magazines and a good novel. With my cluster of fluffy pillows waiting, I lit a small candle on my nightstand and put on some soft background music. Best of all, I gave myself permission to stay put for a while. Occasionally indulging in this perfect morning fantasy feels like a little piece of heaven on earth.

One day soon, why not treat yourself to breakfast in bed, either alone or with your sweetie? Keep it as simple as possible because the whole idea is to spend time relaxing in bed, not cooking in the kitchen. Serve in-season fresh fruit topped with yogurt or cream. If you're feeling ambitious, bake a fruit cobbler the night before. Or try toasted English muffins with strawberry preserves, pumpernickel toast with apple butter, or quiche with spinach and cheese. Another favorite is cranberry muffins spread with honey-lemon butter, which you can make yourself by adding a little honey and lemon juice to some softened butter. Whatever you choose, remember that you want limited knife and fork activity. When it's kept simple, I can't think of a more delightful way to practice innocent pleasures.

START YOUR DAY REFRESHED

The morn is up again, the dewy morn,
with breath all incense, and with cheek
all bloom, laughing the clouds away with
playful scorn, and glowing into day.

LORD BYRON

If you have a difficult time relating to Byron's description of morning, you're not alone! When people are asked why they get out of bed every morning, most say it has more to do with needing to go to the bathroom than with viewing the grandeur of dewy grass or clouds being laughed away. Aside from that, many folks admit it takes them an hour or more to feel alert once they are up. Others can't remember getting dressed or how they got to work! Some people feel sleepy all day and have felt that way for so long that they can't remember what it's like to be truly awake.

One key to greeting the day with enthusiasm and energy is to practice pleasurable routines first thing in the morning. For starters, let the daylight in by leaving the drapes or shades partly open. Allow nature to work her marvelous wonders. In the days before electricity, sleep cycles were regulated naturally by the rising and setting of the sun. By shutting out the daylight, we hinder what should happen naturally. Once you're up, open the shades wide and turn on some bright lights to jump-start your body into "awake mode."

The mind and soul seem especially sensitive to sounds during the period when you're just waking up, so avoid the angry buzz of the alarm by using a clock radio. Wake up to music by not setting the alarm on the hour or half hour (to avoid the news). Or pop in an inspirational message on audio-cassette. To make the transition from one world to another, take a little time to nestle under the sheets. Snuggle under the covers for a few moments while you envision your day going beautifully. If you're not alone, spend a few minutes cuddling your sweetie.

Once you're awake, have a slow, luxurious, full-body stretch. (Watch the way your pets do it!) Arrange to have something special waiting for you—a jug of freshly squeezed orange juice in the fridge or something fun scheduled first thing on your agenda. Start your day with prayer and expectation. "Let the day have a blessed baptism," said Henry Ward Beecher, "by giving your first waking thoughts into the bosom of God. The first hour of the morning is the rudder of the day."

RESTORATIVE
BATHING RITUALS

*I can't think of any sorrow in the world that
a hot bath wouldn't help just a little bit.*

Susan Glaspell

f I'm having a hard time getting up, I often have a candlelight bubble bath first thing in the morning! It may seem extravagant and self-indulgent to even imagine yourself luxuriating in a tub full of bubbles so early in the day, but let's face it—it doesn't cost much, nor take a lot of time.

While you're at it, serve up your morning coffee or English breakfast tea in your prettiest china cup rather than that stained old mug. Enjoy some freshly squeezed orange juice in a stemmed crystal goblet while you relax in the water. When you're ready, dry off with an oversized fluffy towel (one that's been warmed in the dryer), massage in some rich lotion, snuggle up in a terry cloth robe, and bask in your feeling of well-being.

Restorative bathing practices are age-old. Napoleon Bonaparte used to retreat to a piping hot bath during the middle of the night. Katherine Hepburn is known to take up to five baths a day. Apparently Winston Churchill took more than that during high-stress times in his career (an unusual way to deal with a crisis!). While it may not always be convenient to get in a tub, you might be able to manage a hand or foot bath. Fill a basin with warm water and add a few drops of rosemary or sage essential oil or chamomile tea for a comforting effect.

If you're at work and dealing with a particularly stressful situation, take a short break and massage your hands while holding them under very warm running water for a few minutes. It provides incredible results, and the effects are immediate. Finish by drying your hands briskly with a towel and applying soothing lotion. Enjoy the restorative benefits, and feel stress and anxiety being washed down the drain.

If this sounds frivolous, remember that you're caring for yourself by adding enchantment and innocent pleasures to everyday activities. Besides, nurturing yourself is one of the nicest things you can do for the other people in your life. They will thank you for it when they see how calmly you handle the rest of the day.

THE MORNING SHOWER—
ALIVE, AWAKE, AND ALERT!

*I will cause showers to come down in their
season; there shall be showers of blessing.*

EZEKIEL 34:26

ater has a rejuvenating effect on all living things.
Trees and flowers perk up after a rain shower.
Plants are fortified and invigorated when they've
been watered. And after a shower, we are too.

First thing in the day, choose to spend some time consciously appreciating the benefits of this marvelous stimulator.
As you let warm water cascade down your body, revel in it,
listen to it. Feel the blood rushing to all your organs and cells.
There's energy in moving water. As it vigorously pounds and
bounces off your skin, it wakes up your whole body.

If you really want to stimulate the nerves, try turning from
hot to cold water—gradually, of course. Remember, warm
water relaxes and cool water revitalizes. You don't want to
shock your system, but by going slowly from very warm to
very cool, your entire body comes alive. And don't just stand
there! Use a loofah or bathing brush to scrub your body.
Then start jiggling and bouncing. Keep moving. This is a
habit I started a number of years ago when the idea was first

introduced to me. Now my family enjoys the benefits as well. In our house, you can always tell when someone in the shower has just turned from hot water to cold because of all the dancing, jumping, and yelping going on! It's the next best thing to plunging into a cool lake after a relaxing sauna.

As you towel dry, continue the benefits by rubbing your skin briskly and thoroughly. Smooth on some body lotion and tell each part of your body that you love and appreciate it. When you get in the habit of starting each day this way, you'll feel better, look better, and have a happier, healthier outlook.

HIDE OUT FOR A DAY

Remember, the day's events will unfold
whether you're available or not.

Perhaps you've told yourself, "Once I get this next project completed, I'll take time off" or "I know it's important, but I have too many responsibilities." If you're like me, when you attempt to hide under the covers for a day, your inner critic says, "What are you doing here? You're supposed to be working!" Yet, if everything must be in perfect order before we allow ourselves a day off—desk cleared, errands complete, newspapers read, gardens manicured, laundry folded, bills paid—we'll never experience one of the great secrets of contentment: *free time!*

Play hooky one day and arrange a retreat for yourself. Some companies grant special time off as mental health days. Even if you don't have that luxury, carve out some time. It doesn't have to be a full day. Could you leave work early one Friday? Take a Saturday morning off? Skip an evening event you weren't looking forward to anyway? Then cancel the guilt trip and give yourself permission to hide with no timetables, no lists, no clocks, and no expectations.

To know what your needs are, listen to your heart and create your personal *joy list*. Jot down some of the pastimes that would let your dream of a day of comfort come true. Make sure what you choose is relaxing and refreshing. Your ultimate goal is complete inner contentment.

Try waking up to your favorite music. When you're up and about, spend time outdoors on your patio, on a balcony, or in a nearby park. Go inside whenever you feel like it. Eat what you enjoy when you feel hungry. Stock the cupboards ahead of time with comfort foods. For me that's pancakes with maple syrup, toasted cheese sandwiches, macaroni and cheese, and chocolate brownies drizzled with fudge sauce! Brew a pot of Swiss almond coffee or make a cup of steaming cocoa topped with real whipped cream and shaved chocolate. Just for a day, ignore the words *fat-free*, *low cal,* and *decaf.*

Spend the whole day in your robe and slippers or in bed with a novel, some crossword puzzles, your journal, and a good pen. Surround yourself with things that make you feel cozy and rested: treasures from a vacation, scented candles, a tape of nature sounds, a crackling fire. Keep a soft, flannel blanket or downy comforter nearby, along with a stack of fluffy pillows for napping.

If this sounds a little too indulgent, try it and see the difference it makes when you return to your schedule. The rewards are priceless.

TRY YOUR HAND
AT CREATIVITY

*Painting for me has always been a spiritual
thing. You are alone with your Creator, and
you have this sense of the love of God who
created you and gave you these gifts.*

TRICIA ROMANCE

Whenever I am creating, my heart connects with this deeply felt expression of a great artist. Even as I write these pages, I am aware of God's voice giving inspiration and guiding my hand in much the same way a parent's hand directs the child who desperately wants to learn how to sketch or print. You may have thought only those blessed with a special gift can ever experience creativity, but the truth is that you were born a creative being. Inside you there's an artist you may not know about.

Most of us don't think of ourselves as real artists. But an artist is simply someone who is able to access the creative energy within. See yourself as an artist—you'll begin to express yourself in unique ways you never thought possible whether you are destined for world fame or not! You have nothing to lose but the misconception that you're not creative.

For some people, art comes in the form of exquisite handicrafts like crocheting, knitting, embroidery, needlepoint, rug hooking, weaving, and quilting. For others, it's found in flower arranging, calligraphy, woodworking, doll making, and home decorating. Writing is my main expression of creativity, but working in my kitchen is also an art form for me when I'm preparing a colorful plate of green broccoli, orange carrots, and red tomato slices. Just the sight of this display of nature's brilliant colors inspires me.

To ignite your creativity and prime the pump of inspiration, take time to visit art galleries and craft shops. Or window-shop and admire the artistic displays. Browse through a fabric store and flip through a pattern book. Envision the possibilities. While you're there, buy a bit of lace to add to a pantry shelf or some quilted remnants to try your hand at making place mats. Visit an art store and pick up some materials to fill a "creative basket" with colored pencils, gold and silver pens, felt markers, a deluxe box of Crayola crayons, glue, watercolors, paper in vivid colors, ribbon, and some modeling clay. Then revel in an exhilarating exercise of creativity—you may surprise yourself.

To create is one of our deepest longings, and in creating we are joined with our Creator. You aren't too old to become accomplished at some form of art or craft. As George Eliot commented, "It's never too late to be what you might have been!"

COME ASIDE
AND REST A WHILE

*A nap is as refreshing
as rain to a fading rose.*

AUTHOR UNKNOWN

*D*o you feel guilty at the thought of taking a nap? In truth, this innocent pleasure puts you in good company. Jesus urged His disciples to "come aside...and rest a while" (see Mark 6:31). Some of the most prosperous, productive, and proficient people in the world, including Winston Churchill, Johannes Brahms, Napoleon Bonaparte, Margaret Thatcher, and Thomas Edison, were known to take time for relaxation in the middle of the day.

When you think of it, napping is an intrinsic part of our natural human rhythm. It's one of the last behaviors we give up when leaving babyhood and one of the first we return to when we become seniors. It's during those crucial years in between that we deny our personal sleep needs. "Caught napping" should be an encouragement, not an accusation! Research has shown that a brief nap can improve everything from moods, memory, judgment, and creativity to communication skills and workplace safety. Fortunately, many businesses now recognize the positive results of the afternoon snooze and provide the opportunity. In some cases, they even have "nap rooms" for employees.

Revisit your views on rest. Schoolchildren need recess. Other cultures take siestas. Machinery needs downtime. Fields need to be left uncultivated for a season. Even God Almighty took one day for rest. So why do we think we can go on endlessly without granting ourselves even a few minutes to recuperate?

For years I relied on caffeine to get me started again when I felt groggy in the afternoon, but then I didn't feel my best. Finally, I learned that allowing myself the "luxury" (now I know it's a necessity) of regularly drifting off for a few minutes lets me do quality work during the rest of the day.

Whether you nap in a chair at your desk, on a chaise lounge under a shady tree, on a porch swing, in a hammock, or wrapped in a cozy quilt in front of a blazing fire, snooze whenever and wherever you can. Relish your naps. Luxuriate in them.

If you don't come apart and rest a while, you may just plain come apart! As Max Eastman commented, "I don't know why we are in such a hurry to get up when we fall down. You might think we would lie there and rest for a while."

ENJOY MASSAGE PLEASURES

> *Whoever is happy*
> *will make others happy too.*
>
> ANNE FRANK

One of the most pleasurable and practical ways to reawaken your sense of touch is through massage. Combined with soothing music, soft lighting, and aromatherapy oils, massage benefits the whole person—body, mind, and soul. The smooth, working rhythm of massage relaxes muscles, releases tension, promotes improved circulation, and cleanses the body of toxins.

When I started building my speaking and writing career, I dreamed of treating myself to a monthly therapeutic aromatherapy facial and body massage. My first experience was euphoric. I left totally relaxed, remarkably exhilarated, and permanently hooked! That night I slept serenely and undisturbed. For days afterward I was more energetic than I'd been for months. Now I budget for it and treat myself to a massage as often as I can. To me, it's a form of preventative maintenance that's vital to my peace of mind and sense of well-being.

Consider a massage anytime you are feeling sluggish, overwhelmed, or overextended. As your muscles are being manipulated, enter into the experience with total abandon. Relinquish any concern about having someone touch you. A professional massage allows you to take without worrying about having to give anything back.

We know that touch can be the difference between life and death for babies. Newborns need to be touched often, and massaging an infant regularly can produce incredible results. Even the natural cuddling and nuzzling between mother and infant forms an amazing bond that carries on through the years. Studies report that toddlers who get daily ten-minute rubdowns are more alert and responsive and sleep better at night.

Massage is an overhaul for the whole body that also discharges toxins and releases endorphins, resulting in a feeling of well-being. If you've never indulged in a massage, don't waste another moment! The inner peace and renewed energy you will experience far outweighs the time, effort, and expense involved.

GIVE YOURSELF
A MASSAGE

*Be thine own palace,
or the world's thy jail.*

JOHN DONNE

f you spend a lot of time alone or are dealing with considerable stress and can't get to a massage therapist often enough, you can practice self-massage. Start with your face. Rapidly rub your hands together until they feel warm. Then place them on your forehead, temples, or cheekbones. Hold your hands still for a few seconds, then rub them in a circular motion. Massage all around your ears and down along the jawbone.

Then move to the scalp. Using peppermint essential oil provides an invigorating, luxurious treat for the scalp and hair. Position your fingertips at your back hairline and, with dime-size circular movements, work over the entire scalp until you reach the front hairline. With a rhythmic motion, move slowly toward the center and back again, this time applying deep pressure. Bring your fingers down to the midpoint of the back of your neck and stroke in a circular direction. Finish off by tapping vigorously all over your scalp. Continue with a facial or by simply washing your face with a textured washcloth and warm water.

And since your hands continually get a workout, whether at the keyboard, in the garden, on the steering wheel, or on the golf course, give them a treat by holding them under warm running water for a few minutes. Squeeze one hand with the other in firm, five-second grips. With gentle pressure, wring each finger and thumb from its base to its tip. Next, press your thumb into your palm for four seconds at a time, progressively working your way across the width of the hand.

For stiff necks and tender shoulders, try rolling a tennis ball between your back and the sofa, wall, or floor. To massage your feet, roll them in a basin filled with marbles.

You may want to exchange massages with your sweetie. Heighten the experience by adding massage oils, a few candles, and your favorite music. Be prepared to enjoy what might come next!

LIGHTEN UP

*I pray you...your play needs
no excuse. Never excuse.*

WILLIAM SHAKESPEARE

t the end of my seminar "Living Stress-Free in the Midst of Chaos," I give each participant a red clown nose. In one program, I encouraged a group of male executives to wear them, but while a few agreed, most had to be prodded. Finally, one by one they loosened up. Some even cavorted on tabletops, proudly displaying their new look to the entire group. These fellows turned into the most animated, energized, and enlivened bunch of executives I had ever worked with!

Sometimes we get so grown-up that we lose our ability to play. Humor and fun are natural. If nothing in life is amusing, perhaps we've buried our intrinsic passion for play. Children operate mostly from the right side of their brains, the creative, artistic, intuitive hemisphere. Schooling may overemphasize the left hemisphere, which is the analytical, logical, learning center. Continuing to use both hemispheres is often referred to as "whole-brain thinking" and leads to balanced living. Leaving the right brain behind robs our daily existence of play. Life becomes tough, tedious, and tiresome. Overly serious adults run the risk of workaholism, stress, and illnesses.

The good news is that it's never too late to have a happy childhood. I remember an interview with a woman who was celebrating her one hundredth birthday. Hoping to determine how she had remained so vibrant, healthy, and energetic, the interviewer asked about her fitness regimen, diet, and mental outlook. Nothing seemed particularly remarkable until she was asked if she'd had a happy childhood. She responded, "So far, so good!" In other words, like Peter Pan, she believed she should never, never grow up.

If you're craving time off, feeling overwhelmed, or simply aching for a temporary escape from the daily grind, give yourself permission to amuse yourself in the pleasures of unabashed silliness! Indulge yourself and let go of the inhibitions about appearances that would hold you back. Lighten up!

PLAY MORE

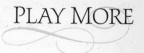

*In every real man a child is
hidden who wants to play.*

FRIEDRICH NIETZSCHE

o you know how to play? Children do it intuitively,
but many people leave this innocent pleasure behind
on the path to adulthood. Some become too mature
and dignified. Others play only to win, not to simply have fun.

Playing "just for the fun of it" is hard for most adults. When
our grandchildren came along, I felt justified once again in
romping, rollicking, and roughhousing; in buying games,
puzzles, and building blocks; and in taking time to do nothing
but be silly. Now I know I don't need an excuse to make
playing a part of my life! In fact, if I want to flourish as a writer,
speaker, and human being, it's essential that I respect the diversion that play offers. Playing for fun provides extraordinary
freedom and a temporary escape from reality—crucial for creativity and well-being.

Watch children genuinely celebrate life with their games and
antics. I remember our children's delight as they gathered adults
together to present a variety show on a makeshift stage. These
days, my husband and I enjoy watching our grandchildren

spend hours playing make-believe in a tent made from blankets draped over chairs or exploring the woods in our backyard.

Children have the capacity to plunge into life with a sense of awe and wonder. Perhaps it's time to reactivate those marvelous feelings of childlike pleasure. Whether it's riding a merry-go-round, building a sand castle, making mud pies, having a squirt gun fight, rolling down a grassy hillside, watching fireworks, or enjoying the swings, slide, and teeter-totter at a local park, play is a marvelous diversion from the stressors of life. In fact, good, frolicking, let-down-your-hair fun is essential for mental, physical, emotional, and spiritual health.

So plan a trip to the circus, have a snowball fight, create a daisy chain, roller skate on a sidewalk, play hopscotch, make angels in the snow, go for a hayride, or fly a kite. Find a symbol of playfulness—a picture of frolicking puppies, a clown sticker, a red balloon, a happy-face pin—and keep it with you. View each day as a breathless voyage of discovery. As Mae West reminded us, "You're never too old to become younger!"

SWEET DREAMS

I will both lie down in peace, and sleep.

PSALM 4:8

leep is an innocent pleasure that helps you stay young and healthy. Studies show that well-rested people age less quickly, live longer, and have healthier immune systems for fighting disease. A good night's rest also affects your frame of mind because that's when the brain replenishes its supply of neurotransmitters, the chemicals that regulate your moods. When you're rested, your metabolism is more efficient and burns more fat. Long-term memory also improves and you can master skills more quickly.

Despite the many advantages of sleep, all too often we go to bed feeling restless. Then we toss and turn all night and wake up needing a good sleep. It's as though our sleep patterns are all mixed up. Wouldn't it be wonderful to know you could lay your head on your pillow tonight, drift off at once into a deeply refreshing sleep, and awaken revitalized tomorrow morning? With some significant lifestyle changes, you can get the shut-eye you've only dreamed about.

Purposely quiet your mind with a period of relaxation before going to bed. Dim the lights early, turn off the television, stay away from your computer, and avoid reading anything thought provoking. This may seem obvious, but for years I stimulated my mind with inspirational books before trying to go to sleep. Ambitious planning or problem solving right up until bedtime will keep you awake. Instead, fill your evenings with soft music and easy reading. Dress in comfy clothing.

Just like children, adults benefit from rituals that trigger the mind to go to sleep. Remember changing into cozy pajamas, brushing teeth, turning down the covers, having a bedtime story with a cup of warm cocoa, and saying prayers?

Try taking a warm bath, lighting a candle, and listening to the same soothing music each night (the secret to rituals is repetition). Choose something comfortable to lounge in, sip a steamy cup of herbal tea, and offer up a good-night prayer of thanksgiving. Just before lights-out, tell yourself that you will have a restful night's sleep and that tomorrow is brimming with wonderful opportunities. Quiet the inner voice that tempts you to concentrate on the obstacles of today or the limitations and uncertainties of tomorrow. Focus on the solutions and possibilities that will come after a good night's rest. Sweet dreams!

PART 2

COME TO YOUR SENSES

SAVOR THE SILENCE

True silence is the rest of the mind;
it is to the spirit what sleep is to the body:
nourishment and refreshment.

WILLIAM PENN

While strolling on our country property one evening, my husband leaned over and whispered in my ear, "Listen!" Since I didn't hear a thing, I asked him what he wanted me to hear. "The quiet," he said. And when I heard it, I found it almost overwhelming. Most of us have become so accustomed to the cacophony of sounds around us that until our attention is drawn to its absence, we're not aware of how much it invades our space. Beyond that, we sometimes get so used to the lack of silence that we can be uncomfortable when faced with it.

Silence eliminates all distractions, pulls our attention inward, and compels us to be alone with ourselves. Have you ever said, "It's so noisy I can't hear myself think"? Silence, stillness, and solitude allow you to discover your most profound and meaningful inner pleasures. To hear on this deep internal level, we have to periodically escape the external racket. Mother Teresa told us, "We need to find God, and He cannot be found in noise and restlessness. God is the friend of silence."

Try to remember the last time you had even 15 minutes of complete silence (not counting sleep time). We live in a noisy world. We wake up to the nerve-rattling bellow of the alarm clock. Then comes the hum of the electric toothbrush or roaring blast of the hair dryer. The television blares while we dress and eat, and we drive to work listening to the babble of morning talk shows and the blaring of horns honking in rush-hour traffic. Our work days are filled with ringing telephones, the din of office equipment, and sounds of people talking. Even on weekends we're subject to the clamor of lawn mowers, leaf blowers, and our neighbors' festivities.

Create silence in your own world. Try waking up without an alarm by envisioning yourself waking up at whatever time you choose. You may already be waking up just before the alarm goes off. Occasionally go without the TV and stereo, or leave the radio off when you're in the car. Walk and exercise without listening to audiotapes. Turn off the phone and let the answering machine pick up messages. Just as carpets, heavy drapes, and foam pads under small appliances muffle clatter, silence creates insulation between you and the loud, demanding world you live in. Bask in the pleasure of silence. The quiet hush may seem peculiar at first, but eventually you'll come to cherish this innocent pleasure.

THE JOY OF LISTENING

*I wonder if anyone else has an ear so turned
and sharpened as I have, to detect music,
not of the spheres, but of the earth....*

KATE CHOPIN

While silence is priceless, and it is helpful to learn how to tune out bothersome noise, we don't want to miss the sounds that nourish and comfort us. Occasionally we become so accustomed to certain sounds that we no longer hear them. This can be good if you live near a railroad crossing, or, like me, have a gun club located directly behind your property. In other instances, our ability to tune out may be what communication experts refer to as "selective listening." By doing so, we lose our ability to really listen to one another, to our inner voice, and to the sweet, soothing sounds all around us.

Once you've turned off the stereo, TV, and car radio, train your ears to listen. Stand still, close your eyes and notice the farthest and closest noises you can make out. Be conscious of your emotional reaction to them. Soon you will begin to once again discern the pleasurable sounds that were there all along: a distant train whistle, leaves rustling in the breeze, happy voices of children playing next door, birds singing at backyard feeders.

In summertime, I am soothed by the wind chimes on my back porch, the wooden screen door slamming, and the creaking of a wicker rocking chair. In winter, these are replaced by logs crackling in the fireplace, the teakettle's whistle as I anticipate a welcome break, and popcorn popping to enjoy with a game of Scrabble.

You may find that sounds of home are comforting—the family dog barking, the baby's sweet voice cooing from her crib in early morning, a son's car pulling into the driveway, your hubby's key in the door, children giggling at play, or the antique clock ticking down the hall. Nature sounds are also particularly nourishing. Listen to a bullfrog croaking, crickets singing, the loon calling from across a lake, rain on a roof, and the wind blowing. Environmental sound recordings work well when you can't get out into nature, and they also effectively mask unwanted noises.

When your heart and soul need a hug, or if you are feeling tired, stressed, and frazzled, soothing sounds will release tension, lift your mood, and energize your spirit.

THE SOUNDS OF MUSIC

Music is well said to be
the speech of angels.

THOMAS CARLYLE

*M*usic can have a profound effect on our moods—it can lift us from the deepest doldrums, shake the blues away, maintain a good attitude, and relax and rejuvenate us. So, if you need a rush of joyful energy and exhilaration, listen to a few minutes of boogie-woogie on the radio.

Besides being a marvelous source of pleasure and an entertaining diversion, music can be a dynamic restorative force. Musical therapy has been practiced for centuries. Today, hospitals use music for everything from helping parents relax during childbirth to preparing patients for surgery. Listening to music produces a total body response, including increasing blood volume and decreasing heart rate—unless, of course, it's a dance beat! Could this be what Emily Selinger meant when she proclaimed, "What joy to capture song from sound and send it throbbing through the hearts of men"? Perhaps this explains the profound healing power of some forms of music, especially favorite old hymns and cherished gospel songs. I still find comfort in the ones I learned as a child: "Amazing Grace," "The Old Rugged Cross," and "In the Garden."

Whether you're looking for a healthy distraction from worry or you need a surge of creativity, there's music to match every mood and event. As a child, I fell asleep each night while my dad played music from the big band era on his piano. Gentle piano nocturnes by Frédéric Chopin or Robert Schumann can calm frazzled nerves, mend a heartsick soul, and pacify a fussy baby. Latin music, or anything with an upbeat tempo, brings cheer and boosts enthusiasm. Stringed instruments, woodwinds, and a slower tempo can help you unwind. Maybe that's why those songs are some of our favorites. Jazz or swing works well when you're cooking or cleaning, classical music gets creativity flowing, and lively show tunes or movie soundtracks keep us inspired.

How long has it been since you've really listened to the music that moves you and speaks to the depths of your soul? Take a few moments to become immersed in a flood of your favorite sounds just as you would soak in a warm, soothing bath. Be saturated in the melody and cleansed by its splendor—you'll emerge restored.

CREATE A
NOURISHING TAPE

Music is what feelings sound like.

AUTHOR UNKNOWN

*O*n a day when you're feeling energetic, healthy, and in a positive frame of mind, make a "nourishing" tape for yourself that you can listen to when you need a boost. Record selections of music you find especially comforting, soothing, or uplifting. Then tuck the tape away and bring it out when you're feeling dreary, lonely, discouraged, or exhausted.

What is it about music that touches our soul? Oscar Wilde called music "the art which is most nigh to tears and memory." Even the fragment of a line is brimming with recollections and can unlock a storehouse of memories. Perhaps that's why I cherish one section of my nourishing tape more than others: a recording my father made for his parents to commemorate their fiftieth wedding anniversary. After making a few introductory comments congratulating them, he then played the piano in the grand style that was his alone. The songs he chose created an intimate and touching life review for my grandparents. Using music that was popular throughout their relationship, he took them on a musical journey, starting with their courtship, right through the war, the year their only child was born, the time they bought their first home, and on through the entire 50 years. Between songs, my father spoke affectionately to his parents, commenting on each era and its corresponding piece of music while sharing his own impressions of life at each stage. What an incredibly moving and romantic gift that goes on long after his death and theirs.

When making your tape, include your favorite music, restorative and invigorating quotes, and soothing poems. Consider integrating telephone messages left by special people in your life. I love to listen to the sound of my husband's voice whenever he leaves me a message, and also those of our grandchildren—especially when they were toddlers and just beginning to babble. Add a few comedy routines, encouraging affirmations, and inspiring Scripture verses, and you've got a personalized inspirational tool that can bring you out of the doldrums.

DELIGHT IN THE MIRACLE OF TOUCH

*The first sense to ignite,
touch is often the last to burn out.*

Frederich Sachs

ouch can have a profound effect on many aspects of our lives. We find comfort at birth in a mother's arms, and at death, in the gentle clasp of a loved one's hand. Yet we often overlook this essential life element and immense source of enjoyment.

One evening, I realized all over again the innocent pleasure of touch while my husband and I sat together reading. When I reached over and caressed his hand, his skin felt exceptionally dry. I left to find some moisturizing cream and came back to massage it into his free hand. When I looked up from what I was doing, he had stopped reading and seemed startled by this gesture. I was surprised at his tender reaction; he was clearly moved by my simple touch.

As a little girl, on those evenings when I had a hard time falling asleep, I remember my mom or dad gently stroking my forehead and continuing to "comb" my hair with their fingers until I drifted off into slumber. Whether it's cuddling your children, walking hand in hand with that special someone down a winding country road, experiencing the feel of silk or satin against your skin, caressing your pets, giving someone a fond embrace, or wiping away a tear, physical touch is more than skin deep. Positive touch not only improves our overall sense of emotional well-being and promotes physical healing but also remedies many of the frustrations of our relationships, taking them to a new level of intimacy.

A bumper sticker asks, "Did you hug your child today?" This is a good reminder that touch is something we all need throughout our lives.

SHOW CARING
THROUGH TOUCH

*A handshake, a pat on the back—touch
someone and enjoy the connection.*

Touch is truly our most powerful and intimate form of nonverbal communication in relationships. Even in business and social situations, it's how we show someone we genuinely care. Through my international travels, I have found that people in some cultures are more comfortable with touching than people in others. While a handshake is really the only permissible form of touch for North American business interactions, other places around the world allow an arm around someone, a shoulder pat, or a hug. Sadly, with a growing concern about sexual harassment and abuse, touch has to be strictly monitored for appropriateness. However, even the most casual touch can have a profound effect in a business setting.

In one study, waitresses who touched customers on the hand as they returned change were found to receive more in tips than those who didn't. Politicians know the benefits of handshakes while making their way through the crowds. As I signed the papers after purchasing my first new car several years ago, I began to suffer what is commonly known as "buyer's remorse"—second-guessing the decision I had just made and feeling nervous about the expense. The astute salesman recognized this and reached over to touch my hand across the desk while telling me I was going to be so glad I had chosen those extra options. It may not have eliminated all the fear, but it did get me out the door before I changed my mind.

Look for new ways to share touch with people in your life. In social situations, shake hands more often and greet close friends with a fond embrace. Before a meal, hold hands around the table when you offer thanks. Embrace your children regularly and caress their faces as you snuggle with them. Brush or wash your partner's hair, kiss more often, tickle each other's arms with a feather, and give more hugs. Hold hands on a walk or during a heart-to-heart talk. Appreciate the texture and the warmth of skin. Every time you get the chance, gently squeeze a loved one's hand—three times says "I love you!" Let's enjoy this innocent pleasure and delight in our sense of touch.

THE PAMPERING BATH

*I went at noon to bathe, and floating
on my back, fell asleep. Water is
the easiest bed that can be.*

BENJAMIN FRANKLIN

*F*ew pleasures compare with a relaxing soak in the tub and emerging from the perfect bath soothed and peaceful. The bedtime bath is a calming ritual I have practiced for a number of years. It's an age-old custom that banishes tension and helps me to rebalance and recover a sense of well-being. I like to slip into a tub full of sparkling warm water sweetened with soothing oils or scents. Lavender is particularly calming, and Epsom salts are known for their muscle-relaxant properties. You can scout out aromatherapeutic blends that ease stress, calm moods, and relieve tension.

Indulge occasionally in a candlelight bubble bath. Add a bit of foaming gel to the water and turn off the lights to luxuriate in the flicker of scented candles you've placed around the room and delight in the iridescent bubbles. Add your favorite classical music and a cup of herbal tea or fruit-flavored sparkling mineral water, and you can soak away all your cares—mental, emotional, and physical.

Holding a warm teacup in your hands and feeling the steam rise up from both the cup and the bath provide tremendous comfort. For a particularly tranquil experience, forget the candles and shut out all the lights. Bathing in complete darkness helps you close out everything else and concentrate on the sheer pleasure of the water. Heavy limbs become buoyant, taking the load off muscles and prompting a release of tension. Blood pressure is lowered as the body tries to lose heat by dilating blood vessels at the surface of the skin. Because of the skin's temperature-sensitive nerve endings, your circulation improves as it responds to the soft caresses of warm water.

Lie back on an inflatable pillow, close your eyes, and wipe your mind clean. In your imagination, see all the concerns that accumulated during the day being rinsed away into the comforting, healing water. This is not a time for scrubbing and getting clean but a chance to soothe your body and soul.

SOOTHING SCENTS

*All around us are exquisite aromas that
can spur memories and transform moods.*

bouquet of flowers on your desk, clean sheets on
the bed, a turkey roasting in the oven, freshly cut
grass—familiar scents have the marvelous ability to
trigger pleasant thoughts, soothe our minds, and enliven our
run-down spirits. "For the sense of smell, almost more than
any other, has the power to recall memories, and it's a pity that
we use it so little," Rachel Carson reminds us.

I remember spending summer vacations at the cottage and
waking up to the smells of freshly made toast, coffee, and siz-
zling bacon. Anytime I choose, I can close my eyes and be
instantly transported back to a more carefree place and time. In
other memories, I am surrounded by the comforting scents of
my grandparents' house: the sandbox in the backyard, a cedar
chest, the attic at home, the church where I attended Sunday
school, and the raspberry patch where my girlfriend and I
picked fruit during our teens.

According to researchers, an aroma goes directly to the
brain. Smell is 10,000 times stronger than the other four

senses—our brain registers aromas twice as fast as it does pain. Our sense of smell works with our nervous, respiratory, circulatory, and immune systems and can powerfully transform emotions. Besides stirring memories, smells kindle other senses when we're drowsy, stir our passions, ignite our desires, enchant and delight us, and warn us of impending danger.

To enjoy the restorative comfort and healing properties of fragrance, try sprinkling essential oil on a cotton handkerchief. Then pull it out during the day, breathing in fully, deeply, and slowly to encourage relaxation anytime you need it. Decide to delight in your sense of smell. It's too potent an innocent pleasure to neglect.

THE SCENT
OF A MEMORY

Smells are surer than sounds and sights
to make heartstrings crack.

RUDYARD KIPLING

romas evoke memories and in so doing, influence our emotions. When my father passed away a number of years ago, I developed a special fondness for his favorite Old Spice cologne. The mere scent of it brings a flood of fond recollections, and I am comforted almost as though he were nearby once again. I hadn't realized how much that fragrance was a part of him until the memory of it began to make such an impact.

Take time to focus on some of your most enjoyable scents. Make a mental aroma list, or record your favorite smells in a journal. Consider such aromas as newly turned earth, cinnamon muffins, fresh bread, popcorn, and new books.

If you need a boost to stir nostalgic reflections of pleasant times, create some sensual treats for yourself. Buy a box of crayons, and enjoy the paraffin-and-pigment scent you knew as a child. According to a Yale University study, it's one of the 20 most recognizable aromas to adults. Lie on the grass in your backyard, or turn over some soil in your garden, and breathe in the pungent fragrance. Enjoy a dusting of baby powder after your bath, or spritz on some fruit-scented body spray. Stroll through a bakery or stationery store, or gather some aromatic herb plants at a farmers' market. Take a walk in the woods or your garden right after the rain, and breathe in the scent of moist earth. Visit a secondhand bookstore, and become enveloped in the fragrance of old leather mingled with the sweet scent of musty pages.

Try cooking for smell. Stew apples with cinnamon and cloves on the back burner. Simmer a mixture of mulling spices (cinnamon sticks, whole cloves, allspice, and dried lemon peel) for an hour or so. Occasionally I fry garlic, onions, and peppers in olive oil and add some tomatoes, mushrooms, basil, and oregano to serve on fresh pasta for supper.

Enjoy sweet-smelling flowers, fragrant potpourri, and burning logs in your living room. Use lemon-scented polish on your furniture, or apply vanilla to the bare wood underneath. Imagine the emptiness we would experience if we were suddenly deprived of this innocent pleasure—our sense of smell.

AH, FOOD, GLORIOUS FOOD

What was Paradise? But a garden,
an orchard full of trees and herbs, full of
pleasure, and nothing there but delights.

WILLIAM LAWSON

think that food was created to be one of life's most sumptuous innocent pleasures. But something went awry. Perhaps back when Eve took that notorious first bite of apple, food became our adversary. That bite launched us on a perpetual mission to plan low-calorie, sugar-free, high-fiber, low-fat meals while denying our innermost cravings. We do battle with our eating habits, yet we know that the human body is an energy system that needs efficient food fuel. Food enables us to survive. So, as my husband reminds me on his third trip to the Sunday brunch buffet, if we have to eat to stay alive, why not enjoy it?

We can recapture this innocent pleasure by responding to our hunger with nutritious, restorative foods. Concentrate on choosing foods that are alive. The most appetizing foods appeal to all five senses—taste, texture, smell, sight, and sound. Hear the crunch of a crispy apple. Feel the effervescent fizz of sparkling fruit-flavored mineral water. Observe the brilliant tones in an array of tomatoes, broccoli, and carrots. Relish the flavor of luscious strawberries. Savor the aroma of rye bread fresh from the oven. Then, as you eat, focus your awareness on what's about to go into your mouth. Concentrate on the sensation of your food.

If you worry that eating whenever you're hungry will cause you to end up the size of a house, be thankful you have an appetite. The lack of one can indicate that something is dangerously wrong. Food needs vary from person to person and from season to season, so start listening to your body tell you what it needs. The more you pay attention to your body's messages, the clearer you'll be concerning the best foods for you. When you do, you'll achieve your ideal weight, feel the most vital, have the most energy, and be the most confident.

Our bodies must be nourished, not only physically but also spiritually and emotionally. When we are undernourished in these other areas, we eat to drive away unpleasant feelings. As you nurture your spirit and fulfill your deepest longings with other personal pleasures, food will begin to lose its hold on you. Eating will become the innocent pleasure it was meant to be, satisfying your physical body as other innocent pleasures nurture your mind and soul.

A CELEBRATION
OF TEA

*There is a great deal of poetry
and fine sentiment in a chest of tea.*

RALPH WALDO EMERSON

In my childhood, the phrase "Let's make a pot of tea" could be heard throughout our house whenever there was a hint of shattered nerves. Having a nice cup of tea was the first thing to do when the problems of the world needed to be solved. My mother still says on occasion, "Have a cup of tea and you'll feel better." She seems to believe my spirits will be lifted even though there isn't a problem!

I guess that's why simply saying the word "tea" causes me to sigh with contentment. The thought of holding the piping hot cup in my hand and taking that first sip induces the anticipation of a few moments of peace and tranquillity. Contemplating the pleasure of teatime evokes images of grace, composure, and elegance, and I begin to breathe freely. With the ever-increasing busyness and turmoil all around us, most of us long for and cherish times of quiet serenity and inner contentment. The ritual of tea somehow has the incredible ability to satisfy this yearning.

A cup of tea can be an inner journey as well as an aesthetic experience. Teatime provides restful moments to ponder life's pilgrimage and brings us in closer touch with ourselves. The ceremony of tea provides an opportunity to simply "be" rather than "do." It allows us the chance to meditate, ponder, and mull over the true nature of things. The tea ceremony invites us to think about what is truly important and to see beauty in simplicity. It reminds us that we *can* experience enchantment each day and that quiet elegance must not be forgotten in the pursuit of achievement.

There is more to this fascinating plant we call tea than just leaves. There is more to the ceremony than ornate cups and flowery china pots. Sipping tea restores balance and harmony in our lives. Tea is available to all of us, whether you are planning an afternoon tea party for friends or simply looking for a lift. To me, life is art, and serving tea represents the art of living. The celebration of tea is an innocent pleasure that restores our spirits.

TEA FOR ONE

*There are few hours in life
more agreeable than the hour
dedicated to the ceremony
known as afternoon tea.*

HENRY JAMES

When I travel to Great Britain, I love to take part in teatime. Among the British people this continues to be a leisurely custom. There's afternoon tea, which is usually served with tiny cucumber sandwiches, fancy sweet cakes, and warm scones with Devonshire cream; and high tea, which is served at supper time, featuring more filling, hearty foods and hot dishes. And, when I'm at home, whether I'm alone or with others, I like to live lavishly by reveling in this marvelous tradition. After all, a little self-indulgence now and again is good for the soul. Like taking a late evening bubble bath by candlelight, a celebration of "tea for one" is a soothing, comforting ritual.

Treat yourself to a quiet break in the day by having tea alone. Pamper yourself with all your favorite things: your preferred blend of tea; your favorite biscuit, muffin, or tea bread; your cherished china teapot, cup, and saucer. A friend of mine places a pretty paper doily on the saucer beneath the cup for added grace and beauty. I think I'll try it next time! Arrange your tea and all the paraphernalia on an attractive tray along with a pretty linen napkin and perhaps a small vase of fresh flowers. Add some soothing background music or a beloved book, find a cozy corner, and curl up in your favorite chair. It's in these quiet moments when I retreat from the world that I feel most nurtured and blessed.

If you are an artist or writer, or if you have your office at home, you may be detached from the world for most of the day. Tea is an ideal time to do something social even though you're alone. At teatime you can legitimately walk away from computers, faxes, and answering machines for a time of restoration. When busyness and distractions spin crazily around you, carve out these important yet simple private times for rest and contemplation. Sadly, most corporations lack both set times and places for people to rest quietly.

Teatime helps us experience tranquillity, grace, joy, and serenity, and in doing so, revives our creativity. Tea for one mellows the soul. "While there's tea, there's hope" said Sir Arthur Pinero. With a few sips and deep breaths, this exquisite pleasure begins to transform our spirits.

MARVEL AT
THE HEAVENS

When I consider thy heavens,
the work of thy fingers, the moon and
the stars, which thou hast ordained;
What is man, that thou art mindful of him?

PSALM 8:3-4

Nothing spells out eternity quite like gazing into the sky. Studying the stars is one of the oldest forms of entertainment. This is one innocent pleasure that makes us aware of how small we are and how short our life span is. When we consider the boundless light-years and myriad of galaxies, we are brought face-to-face with the majestic magnitude of God, the Creator of heaven, earth, and our very souls. When we take the time to pause and look up, we remember the comforting words from the campfire song we sang in our youth: He really does have "the whole world in His hands."

To put your life back in perspective, study the sky. Prepare a picnic breakfast and drive to a scenic spot to see the sunrise. Lie in the grass on a lazy summer afternoon to watch fleecy cloud formations. Reflect thoughtfully, or have some creative fun identifying shapes before they change in the breeze. Spread a blanket in the yard on a clear summer night, count the stars, and find one to wish on. During a visit to my sister's home, she and I spent every evening stargazing while floating on our backs in her pool.

Along with the stars, watch for meteor showers! They're like magnificent fireworks displays that light up the sky. The best time to catch them is from August 10 to 13 when you'll possibly spot 65 meteors in an hour. Take a sleeping bag and pillow, and snuggle with a family member under the night sky in your backyard or on the roof. You get to know your family in a new way when you're cuddled together in the great outdoors. Our children still talk about the many summer nights they slept on the balcony of our city apartment.

And look for the smallest lights in the sky: fireflies. Tonight at twilight, my garden was transformed into an enchanting wonderland of twinkling lights as these lightning bugs filled my backyard, while I stood quietly in their mist. Do you remember catching them in a jar with holes punched in the lid and a plush grass carpet in the bottom? One balmy summer evening, do it again. While you're out there, count the chirps that the crickets make and have someone push you on an old tree swing! Ralph Waldo Emerson expressed it well when he said, "At night, I went out into the dark and saw a glimmering star and heard a frog and nature seemed to say, 'Well, do these not suffice?'"

PART 3

NAME YOUR DAYS

NAME YOUR DAYS

To affect the quality of the day,
that is the highest of arts.

HENRY DAVID THOREAU

lthough we have little or no control over many circumstances in life, we can choose how we meet and greet each day. Our good friend and former pastor suggested that we could alter the quality of our days by naming them according to what we hope to experience.

Experiment with how much influence you really have on your day by naming it first thing in the morning. Write out the name, keep it with you, and live the day accordingly. Look for opportunities to apply the name you've chosen as you go about your daily activities. For example, naming a day Carefree or Joyful automatically gives the day (or at the very least, crucial moments of it) a positive flavor. Names such as Thoughtful, Compassionate, Generous, or Caring get us to look outside ourselves to the needs of others. Grateful and Satisfied cause us to ponder and reflect on the good that surrounds us and to count our blessings instead of focusing on unfulfilled wants, plans, and dreams. Naming your day Enthusiasm or Excitement enables you to face daily tasks with a sense of adventure, and calling a day Laughter or Hilarity opens the door to fun, amusement, and lighthearted silliness. Name your day Passionate or Loving and you may be surprised at the tenderness and warmth you experience in your relationships.

You could even name your days according to the letters of the alphabet. For example, the first day might be Affection, the next Beauty, followed by Contentment, and so on, perhaps ending with Zeal.

Although our best efforts and positive attitudes do not guarantee prosperity, perfect health, or inner peace, we have the ability to choose our outlook. Even if we're feeling overwhelmed with frustration, setbacks, grief, illness, or disappointments, choosing a name for each day helps us to look beyond difficult circumstances.

Before you fall asleep tonight, whisper a prayer for tomorrow to be a marvelous day. You might even want to name it ahead of time! Enjoying this innocent pleasure, you will prove that great expectations are often the preludes to splendid days.

LAUGH A LOT

A cheerful heart does good like medicine.

PROVERBS 17:22 TLB

ave you ever noticed how you feel the morning after an evening of fun and laughter? Try to remember the last time you had a hearty laugh, the kind where your face hurt, your sides ached till you thought they'd split, and tears rolled down your cheeks. The next day, you probably felt refreshed, energized, and ready to tackle the world. Even when we're feeling overwhelmed, over-tired, and overworked, laughter has a way of reviving and invigorating us.

Henri Bergson suggested, "Laughter is a corrective force which prevents us from becoming cranks!" Apparently, laughter acts like a tranquilizer without the side effects. With its mood-altering qualities, laughter is a calming, healing, and soothing balm to your soul! As muscles tighten, relax, and tighten over and over again, tension is released. You get the benefits of an internal workout that has been compared to jogging on the inside. It's a bit like a massage for your internal organs and muscles. When you laugh, your brain releases endorphins and a lot of other powerful antidepressant bio-chemicals that contribute to an overall feeling of comfort and well-being.

Instead of waiting for laughter to happen, plan to integrate humor into your life. Organize special laughter dates that include such activities as board games, comedy theater, funny movies, or musicals. Even when you're alone, choose to spend a few minutes each day laughing. It's not always easy, and you may have to pretend at first, but that's okay. Actors tell us that when they fake laughing, they soon begin to experience the same euphoric feeling. Laughing is a choice; humor can be found in nearly every situation.

To kick start your funny bone, start a file for saving jokes, cartoons, comics, and humorous stories. Assemble a personal humor survival kit. Fill it with funny books, videos, comedy recordings, greeting cards, bumper stickers, and anything else that will get you laughing. Keep a book of jokes in your desk drawer for a laughter break, or create a bulletin board plastered with silly pictures, cartoons, and riddles.

When you consciously bring laughter into your life, you heighten your awareness of the funny side of everyday situations. This innocent pleasure heals, comforts, and purifies the soul. No wonder it's been said that "he who laughs...lasts!"

HAVE A LAUGH
AT YOURSELF

*You grow up the day you have
the first real laugh—at yourself!*

ETHEL BARRYMORE

If you haven't had a good laugh at yourself lately, someone else probably has! Seeing the silliness in our own actions sure beats the alternative of putting ourselves down.

I learned this lesson the hard way the first time I spoke to an especially large audience of professionals representing many different organizations. The size of the group alone made me nervous, but I also knew that if I performed well, each attendee could ultimately go back and suggest that their individual companies hire me for future conferences.

A standing ovation at the end of my talk put me on cloud nine. As I stepped off the platform and made my way through the crowd toward the ladies' room to freshen up, a woman in the audience handed me a small piece of paper with something written on it. It wasn't until after I had looked in the mirror and discovered that my detachable shoulder pads had slipped down to the front of my silk blouse, creating the illusion of an unrealistically large bosom, that I looked at her note, which read, "Angels fly because they take themselves lightly."

Wow—how I needed that piece of advice to find enough strength to leave the ladies' room! Have you ever noticed that we put embarrassment and death on the same level, as if they're equal? "Someday," I told myself, "this will be a hilarious story to tell to friends." I just hoped to quickly narrow the gap between the horror of the present moment and the time when it would eventually become funny. Fortunately, I've been able to bring a lot of laughter to many audiences with that story.

While on a plane recently, I sat next to a professional comedian. As we chatted, he confessed to me that much of his material comes from unsettling events in his life that he has transformed into comedy routines. If comedians can turn their embarrassment into laughter, then certainly we can, too. The next time you have an embarrassing moment, a setback, or an outright failure, see how you can flip it around into a funny story. You'll feel better, and you'll look better, too. As Victor Hugo put it, "Laughter is the sun that drives the winter from the human face."

CRY A LITTLE

*There is sacredness in tears. They are not
the mark of weakness but of power.
They speak more eloquently than
ten thousand tongues. They are the
messengers of overwhelming grief, of deep
contrition, and of unspeakable love.*

WASHINGTON IRVING

My daughter's early arrival to pick up our grand-daughter caught me off guard. She had come ahead of schedule just as baby and I had settled ourselves into a comfy old rocking chair after a morning of play with building blocks and teddy bears. As I sang softly to this precious little one, she snuggled into the quilt on my lap, ready to nap. With her sleepy eyes gazing into mine, she thoughtfully studied my lips as I mouthed each word. Tears were streaming down my cheeks—tears that had come without warning as I was suddenly overwhelmed with unspeakable love. I felt almost embarrassed that my daughter should find me in this tender state, temporarily forgetting that there is sacredness in tears and that they are not the mark of weakness. Charles Dickens expressed it best when he said, "Heaven knows we need never be ashamed of our tears, for they are rain upon the blinding dust of earth, overlying our hard hearts."

Yet our society discourages crying, especially in men and boys. Rather than seeing crying as a weakness, why not allow ourselves the comfort of indulging in this natural, healthy form of emotional release and communication? Besides, new research shines fascinating light on the benefit of tears. Crying purifies and cleanses through the release of harmful substances produced during stress. There is a difference between biological tears—the type produced when chopping onions—and emotional tears that we now know carry toxic chemicals from our systems.

Try to remember the last time you had a good cry. It probably left you feeling drained yet invigorated at the same time, similar to the way you feel after hearty laughter or making love. After a good cry, we often fall into a deep sleep and awake refreshed. Crying is nature's way of helping us cope and also has a wonderful bonding effect connecting the people involved. Tears help to keep our bodies free from disease and restore a sense of balance in our lives. William Shakespeare called our tears "holy water." So, for the sake of your health, your sanity, and your relationships, go ahead and have a good sacred sob once in a while.

GROAN FOR YOUR HEALTH

Groan and forget it.

JESSAMYN WEST

When the phone call came to say my father had passed away, I wasn't shocked. We had known he was seriously ill and near death, and the family had been able to gather for one last visit with him in the hospital. But few of us are ever fully prepared for the loss of a loved one, regardless of the circumstances. As I stood in the shower that morning, my grief overwhelmed me. My body seemed to take over and the moaning began instinctively. I stayed under the warm, gentle stream of water and allowed the groaning to continue until relief came. Later, when I was alone in my car, I once more granted myself permission to give in to that form of release.

I believe that releasing the pain in that way helped me to mourn the loss of my father in a healthy way. Since the beginning of time, people have groaned to release tension. When you think of it, we groan instinctively when we yawn and stretch, if we lift something heavy, and after we've eaten a terrific meal. We moan when we're enjoying a great back rub and also in moments of passion or intense lovemaking. In child-birth, women groan spontaneously. Patients emerging from surgery find that moaning helps ease their pain and suffering.

Groaning can ease emotional pain as well. Our culture tends to discourage this helpful response to pain, as if it were a weakness to overcome. It is not. Allow your body to speak through groaning for an effective, simple, and natural way to get relief from pressures of all kinds. Physically, these primal moans involve the entire body in gentle, rhythmic, relaxing activity. Because moans require deep, diaphragmatic breathing, the oxygen supply to all parts of your body increases. Groaning also provides an inner massage by producing strong inner vibrations.

Experiment with primal groans the next time you are upset or hurt in any way. Imagine groaning as your body's voice, releasing aches, frustration, and disappointments. Continue moaning, sighing, wailing, or whatever is helpful for you until you have emptied yourself. Finish with a deep sigh and then sit quietly for a few minutes. Focus on how relieved you feel and the positive benefits you will reap. When one young mother told her sick child, "I know you're feeling ill, but do you have to make so much noise?" the little one replied, "It just feels better when I groan!" Isn't that the truth?

CULTIVATE A GRATEFUL HEART

What a wonderful life I've had!
I only wish I'd realized it sooner.

COLLETTE

nnoying traffic, an indifferent spouse, bad weather conditions, corruption in government—we can always find something to complain about. And when we're not complaining, we can always find someone else who is. Sometimes life situations make it difficult to be thankful and appreciative. However, no amount of complaining seems to change things or make us feel any better.

When I'm in a grumbling mode, the first thing to leave me is my sense of gratitude. Giving thanks is the direct opposite of griping. Both being thankful and complaining are habits we develop that affect the quality of our days. Few things lift a mood of despondency or negativity more powerfully than gratitude.

I believe I can alter the happenings of a day if the first words out of my mouth in the morning are, "This is the day the Lord has made. Thank you for this day; I will rejoice and be glad in it." No, I can't control everything that will happen, good or bad, but I can choose my outlook. As the saying goes, it's either "Good morning, Lord" or "Good Lord, it's morning!"

Try keeping a gratitude journal. Find something to add to it each day. It's really not difficult to create a full inventory of what you are thankful for. Are you healthy? Is there food on your table? Did you complete a project ahead of deadline or have time to walk for 20 minutes a day according to your plan? Perhaps you're grateful for a bright sunny day, a dependable friend, or someone who allowed you to merge into traffic.

If you're stuck, you could begin by being thankful that you *don't* have a paper cut or an ingrown toenail, that it wasn't the transmission after all, or that no one noticed when you dropped a roast chicken on the floor but recovered it before the dog got it (not that it's ever happened to me).

A few years ago, I set a goal of compiling a thanksgiving list with entries equivalent in number to the current year. That first year, I aimed for 1991 entries! I may not always achieve my goal, but it's a sure way to cultivate a gratitude mentality. After all, life has a way of presenting us with greater benefits when we're thankful for even the smallest ones. The more gratitude you express, the more you'll have to be grateful for. Begin and end your day with a prayer of thanksgiving. As Robert Louis Stevenson reminded us, "The person who has stopped being thankful has fallen asleep in life."

COUNT YOUR BLESSINGS

*Those who wish to sing
always find a song.*

SWEDISH PROVERB

Whenever my grandmother caught us grumbling, she admonished, "You should just count your blessings." Grandma believed that the pleasure of owning what we possess is lost by wanting more. Imagine how different life would be if we focused our attention on the blessings we enjoy each day—those we have either forgotten, ignored, or taken for granted.

One summer our family had the privilege of taking part in a program that gives children from New York's inner city a chance to spend two weeks in a rural atmosphere. As I drove our little guest home, he asked, "Is this really your car?" I told him we had three cars and a truck in our family. Then he asked, "What's your house like?" I described our rather modest country home set on two acres of land. "Are you rich?" was his next question. I laughed and told him, no, we weren't.

When we got home, I showed him the room my young daughter had happily volunteered to let him use while he was with us. I started to apologize for the feminine decor with its lace, ruffles, and frills, but he threw himself onto the bed, pro-claiming, "I feel like a king!" Later, during dinner, he related that he and his family lived in just two small rooms and that they sometimes didn't have money for food. As we tucked him in bed that night, he said, "You *are* rich." We smiled, but deep in our hearts, we knew it was true. The question was, were we appreciative?

A good friend once suggested I could use my morning walk to count my blessings. At first, I wondered if I could fill an entire hour. Surely I'd be stymied by blessing number three. I started with the simple things—a comfy bed, food on the table, a warm bath, eyes that see, ears that hear, legs that make my freedom possible—and continued right up to the end of my walk. I also found I could lull myself to sleep at night by counting blessings rather than sheep.

You may be blessed with a child's laughter, a caring spouse, a dependable friend, or a pet that gives you unconditional love. Rather than concentrating on what's missing, put a positive spin on the day, or at least on the moment, by appreciating the treasures you already possess. Take a moment to consider how abundantly God has blessed you.

GIVE YOURSELF AWAY

*You give but little when you give of
your possessions. It is when you
give of yourself that you truly give.*

KAHLIL GIBRAN

As my granddaughter walked through the mall with me one afternoon, I noticed that she stooped occasionally to pick up bits of litter and then threw them in the trash can. This simple and sweetly innocent act got me started, too. Now together we pick up litter on sidewalks, in movie theaters or shops, or anywhere we happen to see it. This habit is just one way to give yourself away.

Often the best gift is a portion of yourself. Whether it's time, talent, or energy, we all have a little something we can give away to increase joy in another's life. One popular bumper sticker encourages us to do "random acts of kindness." Look around you, and you'll notice lots of opportunities to do just that, as well as chances to plan well ahead for other good deeds.

You might offer your neighbor a helping hand by raking leaves in autumn or clearing snow from the walkway in winter. You could volunteer to read to seniors or the blind, care for babies in your church's nursery, or serve dinner at a local shelter. Perhaps you'd like to plant a tree on National Arbor Day. It doesn't have to be in your yard—check with a school, church, or nursing home. Take dog or cat food to the local animal shelter. Run errands, care for pets, do light housework, or prepare a meal for someone who is ill. On a toll bridge, pay for the car behind you, or put money in a stranger's parking meter when you see it's about to run out. Invite someone for dinner when you know they have an especially hectic schedule, or take a fully prepared meal to a friend who is going through a trying time. Become a mentor for a young person or a guardian angel for someone elderly who could use a little company. Share your talents at a school or nursing home: music, art, crafts, photography. Let someone in line in traffic, open the door for a stranger, or hold a baby to give an exhausted young mother a break. When you gaze into that little one's angelic eyes and see the purity and innocence there, your gift returns to you.

There are thousands of ways you can give yourself away, from wallpapering a friend's kitchen to walking their dog. Look around and ask God to inspire you to find someone who may appreciate a good deed. Then plan a strategy to accomplish your goal. It's even better if you can do it secretly, without revealing your efforts to anyone. Besides, it's a well-known truth that you can never give too much away. Although you don't do it for this reason, what you willingly give away often returns—multiplied. In giving of yourself, you may just get a glimpse of heaven!

DREAM A
LITTLE DREAM

*Hold fast to dreams, for if dreams die,
life is a broken-winged bird that cannot fly.*

LANGSTON HUGHES

*L*et me share with you two questions that helped me believe in the beauty of my dreams, planted seeds of possibilities and faith, and changed my life forever.

First, if you could do or be anything in the world, and you knew you could not fail, what would you choose? Would you go back to school, write poetry, open an antique shop, or learn to play the piano? Maybe you would be president of your own company or learn to fly a plane or take a course in oil painting. Would you build a house, a boat, or a houseboat? Would you start a worthy charity? Dream big—the sky is the limit.

Second, if you could create your ideal life, how would you fashion it? In other words, how would you spend each day, where would you live, who would share your life, where would you work, what would you do in your spare time, what hobbies or sports would you be involved in, where would you go on your next vacation?

Get a pen and your favorite journal, and jot down your answers. If your dreams, buried like seeds lying dormant,

81

could be warmed back to life again with the sunlight of your passion, what would you dare to imagine? Or do you hold yourself back from dreaming of a more joyous, rewarding, and exhilarating life, perhaps to elude the inevitable heartache of disappointment or fear of failing? Maybe you haven't allowed yourself to embrace the inner yearnings that tug on your heart because you're not sure you have what it takes to fulfill your deepest longings.

I think the operative word is "dare." It does take courage to allow yourself to even imagine a better life—one of peace, pleasure, accomplishment, contribution, and fulfillment. Allowing yourself to dream is not as easy as it sounds. Being called a daydreamer as a child probably wasn't complimentary, and you let go of some of your dreams because of it. Yet all change begins with a dream.

Today, give yourself permission to imagine what you have only wished or hoped for until now. When you do, dream big with no limits! Ask for divine guidance, and expect to receive it. The Bible tells us we have not because we ask not. God is waiting to be asked to be part of your dreams; help is closer than you think. As Somerset Maugham put it, "It's a funny thing about life: If you refuse to accept anything but the best, you very often get it."

FIND SERENITY
IN NATURE

Let your mind be quiet, realizing the beauty
of the world, and the immense, boundless
treasures that it holds in store.

EDWARD CARPENTER

Go on a treasure hunt: find a secret outdoor hideaway to escape to when your mind yearns to be quiet. When I'm altogether overwhelmed with life, I crave the tranquillity of my private secluded spot. Sitting by the water's edge, resting under the shade of an old oak tree, walking deep in the woods, or laying on the cool grass on a hilltop, I can finally disengage and release the day's burdens. Delighting in the extraordinary beauty and natural grace of the world somehow lightens the load when responsibilities and obligations get too cumbersome to carry around.

"Nature is an aeolian harp," said Novalis, "a musical instrument, whose tones are the re-echo of higher strings within us." Somehow, the untouched beauty of nature resonates with our own creative spirits, inspiring awe and bringing us back into balance. At times, it seems we are divinely escorted by our Creator to some natural place to collect ourselves. Nature holds our attention and keeps us stimulated, but doesn't demand anything in return. Something in the unruffled calm of nature subdues our petty annoyances and tempers our anxieties. All the sights and sounds, textures and smells seem to still us and breathe peace into our souls.

Our society seems to have lost its appreciation of the elegance and splendor of God's creations, but many cultures throughout history have demonstrated great respect for the most basic elements of nature. The simple beauty of a sunset, the softness of a rose petal, the velvety smoothness of a ripe peach, the intricate pattern of a spider's web, the intense colors of an autumn leaf, or the miracle of a butterfly were all to be celebrated. As Goethe proclaimed, "Nature is the living, visible garment of God." Far from being New Age hocus-pocus, appreciating nature is an integral and necessary part of our lives. To be moved and touched by the splendor of nature is to praise the mighty Creator of such glorious marvels.

Make time to enjoy the restorative, healing, and inspirational power of the great outdoors. Let the glories of nature soothe your mind, uplift your spirit, and energize your body. Immersing yourself in nature's pleasures may leave you with fewer material desires and more true joy and contentment.

TAKE TIME TO MEDITATE

Prayer begins by talking to God,
but it ends by listening to Him.

BISHOP FULTON J. SHEEN

rtists tell us that after being intensely absorbed in a painting, they periodically stand back from their work to determine if it's in balance. It's easy to get so absorbed in the painting of our lives that we lose our sense of perspective. Meditation is one way to see clearly what is off course and needs adjustment to get us back in balance.

If the beginning of prayer is talking to God, then listening and reflecting upon what we hear could be our meditation. The word *meditate* conjures up different images for each of us. I used to envision someone sitting cross-legged on a mountaintop chanting with eyes closed, hands folded, and fingers pointing heavenward. Actually, to meditate simply means to dwell on something to the point that you are oblivious to outside distractions and the passing of time. Meditation implies deliberation, studying what's going on in our lives, pondering what we've heard or read, and closely examining our personal viewpoints, beliefs, and attitudes. As Jack Kornfield writes, "To be at peace requires us to be intimate with our sorrows, anger, loss, struggles, desires, pleasures, joys, and happiness."

When was the last time you really listened to your heart? That is where all the great treasures lie. To meditate is to heed the still, small voice within that belongs to the Creator of the universe—that voice that speaks words of love, direction, guidance, and encouragement to us.

Take a moment to find a private spot where you'll be free from distraction. You need breathing space to journey within and ponder what is precious. Put aside any needs you have; the "goal" in meditation is to listen—to God and to your own heart. What you hear may not be obvious at first, but keep listening until it becomes clear.

The most difficult part is tuning out the hullabaloo inside your head. Most of us are not aware of the incredibly vast number of scattered thoughts that flood through our heads each moment: We're out of bread again…don't forget to stop by the post office…Danny needs new shoes…and the list goes on. Choose to consciously empty your mind of the day's concerns.

Sit silently. Listen eagerly. Wait expectantly. Focus on God's goodness and majesty, and attune your spiritual ears. Quiet reflection is an innocent pleasure that gives you the ability to gain a heavenly outlook, to see the world through new eyes. Your heart is changed, and peace follows.

PART 4

INNOCENT ESCAPES

CREATE A PLACE
OF YOUR OWN

*I love to be alone. I never found
a companion that was so
companionable as solitude.*

HENRY DAVID THOREAU

o you have a place to call your own—somewhere no
one will disturb you? Children have their own
rooms. Men often have garages, workshops, or dens
to retreat to. Women may have craft or sewing rooms or a
home office, but often they're public domain. Find a place
where you can get away from daily routines and other people;
make it a sacred spot to spend time on those special activities
that nourish the soul and define character. You might choose a
spare room, a sitting room, or even the corner of a bedroom,
but let others know it's off-limits.

Mine is part of my office. There's a fireplace in one corner
and a baby grand piano, inherited from my grandmother,
across the room. I'll often sit and play a hymn or two before
starting my day. I have a cozy, plaid love seat with big, comfy
cushions that faces a picture window. Beside it, on the floor, is
a basket of some of my favorite books. That's where I can put
my feet up and read, meditate and pray, or simply take in the
view. There's a CD player next to an armchair where I can listen

to inspiring and uplifting music. When I need an energy boost, or just want to be quiet and think, I can go to my haven and know that I will be alone.

One of my readers shared with me how crucial a place of her own was during a difficult time in her marriage. She needed space to breathe during the turmoil, at least until the relationship was on its way to recovery. Her family's sprawling farmhouse sitting on several acres of land was certainly big enough for six people, several pets, and an office for their home-based business. However, she didn't have a place she could call her own, a spot to escape to for comfort even for a short while.

She decided to clean out a small cabin at the back of their wooded property, freshen it with a few coats of paint and chintz curtains, and furnish it with odds and ends she'd picked up at flea markets. Oil lamps flickered warmly in the evenings. A small camping stove was all she needed to make herself a pot of tea or even cook a meal. In this secret haven, she permitted herself to cry or yell, laugh or pray without bothering anyone. She could daydream or write in her journal or just sit peacefully.

Wherever your sanctuary is, it's not a place for working. Rather, it's a happy, secure retreat where you can be alone to ponder, think, get inspired, discover solutions, or merely bask in the silence.

CREATE YOUR OWN TOY ROOM

*The greatest thing in life
is to keep your mind young.*

HENRY FORD

A toy room makes a statement: "Life can be fun!" Surrounding yourself with playthings provides a constant reminder to fill your life with a spirit of youth and spontaneity. Look around your house to seek out the perfect spot for your toys. It doesn't have to be an entire room. It could be a small corner, a closet, or one shelf. Even a storage box covered in wallpaper, a painted wooden chest, or a wicker picnic basket will do as a place to store the toys you'll use to incorporate more enchantment into your life.

To stock your new toy room, go to one of the many five-and-dime or "dollar" stores that are enjoying a revival these days. Pick up additional toys when you're on vacation, or let people know what's now on your gift list for special occasions!

To get you going, think about the following:

- Toys you had as a child that brought you pleasure: jigsaw puzzles, modeling clay, art paper, glue, colorful pens, pencil crayons, fanciful erasers, notebooks and sketch pads, stickers, finger paints, marbles, jacks, Frisbees, jump ropes, a sand pail and shovel, stuffed toys, Silly Putty, a Slinky

- Silly items like water guns, a jar of bubbles with a bubble pipe, a bright yellow rubber duck for the bathtub, a fake plastic nose, Groucho or pop-out eyeglasses (take them with you for the next time you are stopped in traffic or visiting someone who is down in the dumps or in the hospital), comical masks, funny hats

- Things you always wanted but never had—an antique train set, an airplane collection, roller skates, an ornate doll house to furnish and decorate, a giant teddy bear, a porcelain doll

Your toy room could be the place you do crafts, work on hobbies, or display your favorite collection. It could be any-place you store the things that help you reconnect with that part of you that is still a child. Fun with toys creates a deep inner tranquillity. Taking time to retreat with them is an innocent pleasure that reactivates those marvelous feelings of child-like delight.

VISIT YOUR INNER SHANGRI-LA

If you get simple beauty and nothing else,
you get about the best thing God invents.

ROBERT BROWNING

*I*deally, when life has dealt more than we can handle, we could drop everything to enjoy a month's sojourn at a lake, a tropical beach vacation, or a mountain retreat. When we can't afford the time or money to actually go away, we can enjoy the simple beauty of a mental vacation.

For years I have practiced a restorative ritual I call an inner Shangri-la retreat. The term Shangri-la signifies a haven or paradise, a protective sanctuary hidden away from the rest of the world. When you just can't face your circumstances anymore, close your eyes and visualize some wondrous place you'd like to visit. Perhaps you have a favorite spot you long for when you're feeling overwhelmed or disappointed. It may be a cabin in the woods, a beach on a sunny island, or a cottage by a lake. It may even be your version of heaven!

Your place may be real or imaginary, but when you fill in as many details as possible and appeal to all five senses, your subconscious mind experiences an amazingly real retreat.

Consider all the pleasurable sights, sounds, and textures you would find there. What would you smell or taste at your ideal retreat? When I do this exercise, I see myself sitting on the veranda of my aunt and uncle's cottage, where I spent each summer as a girl. In my mind, I hear waves slapping against the shore, wooden screen doors slamming, children's cries of delight as they splash in the lake, and the clink of ice cubes in tall, frosty glasses. My mouth puckers at the thought of freshly made lemonade accompanied by sugar cookies still warm from the oven. The gentle creaking and rhythmic motion of a rocking chair soothes me. I smell popcorn being prepared in anticipation of an evening of fun and games around the huge, old oak dining table. In only a few minutes, I am reliving the joy, delight, and wonder of memories captured forever in my mind. With this innocent pleasure, it's possible to take a trip in a few minutes. Visit as often as you like, and if you get nothing else but the simple beauty of it all, as Robert Browning suggests, you'll get about the best thing God invents.

ARRANGE A MINIVACATION

*Half a loaf is better than
not loafing at all!*

When a full-fledged trip is out of the question, what about a day trip, an overnight getaway, or a weekend outing? A simple minivacation is a delightful pleasure most of us can manage. Simply being someplace else, temporarily escaping your normal environment to see, eat, and do something novel or unfamiliar can cure boredom, relieve stress, ease the pressure of responsibility, and even help heal a broken heart.

On a minivacation, surroundings have a peculiar clarity and significance because we know we won't be staying long. The same time restrictions that limit the length of our stay also cause us to abruptly narrow our focus. We notice even the smallest details of our surroundings because soon we'll be returning home where everything is already familiar. On a short getaway, our senses are enlivened and we soak in the ambience. We capture each experience because we know we'll never see this particular tree, horse, cappuccino mug, or sunset again. Food tastes better, the light is more golden, church steeples are taller, and gardens more splendid. Washing hung on a line appears brighter, and the roadside diner is more picturesque than the one we frequent back home.

Situations that would be annoying at home—the table at an outdoor cafe wobbling on the cobblestone patio, a broken-down bus holding up traffic, pigeons begging for scraps of the pastry we just bought at the local bakery—are more interesting and tolerable on a minivacation. We may have trouble calling up images of the cathedrals, monuments, galleries, and museums we visited on a genuine, full-blown vacation, but we'll always remember the little things we see on a brief getaway. My husband and I will never forget the six dogs we saw on one overnight retreat. They lay in the shade of a huge oak tree in an orderly fashion, resembling the spokes of a wagon wheel. We might not have used up our film had it happened at home.

Whether you choose to spend the night at a quaint bed-and-breakfast in a nearby town, luxuriate for a weekend at a spa resort, or take advantage of an airline's last-minute sell-off package, your minivacation is a chance to go and see and do whatever it is that you never seem to have time for. You will return invigorated and ready to face life's challenges once again.

Welcome
Unexpected
Vacations

Capture stolen moments—those
sanity-saving interruptions that come
unannounced and disguised
as delays in our schedule.

t was the end of the day, and I was in a hurry, chauffeuring the kids to baseball practice. Our rural route led us past vineyards, fruit orchards, and horse farms. I overheard the children in the back seat chattering about the cherry blossoms that looked to them like pink popcorn on the tree branches. As we drove on, they pointed out the silhouette of a black stallion posing nobly on a hillside against the backdrop of a rose-colored evening sky. Because I was more focused on the slow-moving van up ahead, the dirty dishes in the sink at home, and the project that was due the next day, I barely noticed my surroundings. Not until it was too late did it cross my mind to take a few moments to admire, along with my daughters, the sun sinking slowly into the horizon.

Having missed something so magnificent, I started to think about the many unanticipated vacations that regularly present themselves to us—opportunities to take a break from the mundane hustle and bustle of everyday life. Recognizing that these sabbaticals are often God-given for our benefit should give us reason enough to pause, reflect, and enjoy a moment of peace. Unplanned vacations enrich our days when we give ourselves permission to revel in them.

The minutes spent in a waiting room, at a restaurant, or at your child's music lesson don't have to be merely bothersome delays in your schedule. Capture the moments to browse through a magazine you normally wouldn't have time for or catch up on a book you've been wanting to read. Bring along some small note cards and jot a "thinking of you" note to someone special. Use the time stuck in a line at the store, bank, or gas station to think your own thoughts. In your mind, plan your next vacation. Decide on the menu for an upcoming dinner party or a fun agenda for the evening. Think in advance of some creative ways to spend waiting time. Make those moments fun, not frustrating.

Do you remember "snow days," those excuses to lounge till noon in your pajamas while sipping hot cocoa topped with marshmallows and cinnamon? If you had a fireplace, you might have kept a fire going all day as you played Scrabble, Monopoly, and other board games. Later on, you went sledding or made snowmen. Look for a chance to do it again, and learn to luxuriate in those unexpected vacations.

PLAN AN IMAGINARY TRIP

*Imagination is the
highest kite one can fly.*

LAUREN BACILLI

f you could travel anywhere in all the world, and you knew money was not a concern, where would you go? Would you explore an exotic Caribbean island or take a train ride through the mountains? Perhaps your dream is to go on a Mediterranean cruise, an Oriental junket, or an African safari. Your ideal trip may be an escape getaway to an isolated cabin in the woods or a charming country inn with evenings spent lounging in front of a crackling fire. You might prefer a more action-oriented excursion at a horse ranch, or maybe a ski chalet, fishing lodge, or golf and tennis resort is more to your liking. Whether your ultimate vacation includes something as sensational as a wildlife viewing tour or more placid activities such as riding a biking trail, basking on a powder white beach, or a day full of pampering, this is your imagination, so go ahead and be as outlandish or indulgent as you want to be.

Then, with the power of visualization, fill in all the details in living color. If you need inspiration, start a collection of travel information. Write for brochures, pick up travel guides, seek out maps at a used book store. Hang a poster or colorful collage you've created in plain view. Rent travel videos about foreign countries or out-of-the-way places. Stop in at the library to peruse the travel section. Save postcards sent by others who visited some of your favorite spots, and display them where you'll see them often. Surround yourself with visual reminders to keep the spark of adventure alive.

Don't limit yourself because you don't believe you could afford such a trip. God, the greatest Creator of all, has imparted to you an incredible imagination. Why go economy class? Make this armchair vacation nothing less than a first-class excursion! Besides, who knows? Sometimes focusing on something with intense emotion eventually makes it reality. Some of your imaginary trips may materialize. However, whether or not you ever take it, you'll benefit from planning your dream trip by allowing your imagination to escape the daily grind.

So many marvels in our world await your discovery! Through books, travel guides, maps, videos, and your imagination, get away for a while. When you do, you'll return refreshed.

INDULGE IN A
MIDDAY SNOOZE

*Naps are the adult
version of a child's fort.*

SARK

The vacations I've enjoyed most over the years share one common denominator that arouses in me the most peaceful of memories: the innocent pleasure of napping. Lazy afternoons spent lounging at the water's edge, hidden under a beach umbrella or tucked beneath an enormous straw hat, book in hand…the reading rarely lasts more than a few minutes! The warmth of the sunshine melts away all cares, and balmy breezes caress both body and soul. It's never long before my head nods, the book drops, and deep, nourishing sleep takes over. The best part for me is simply knowing that it's permissible. I allow myself to drift off into oblivion without the guilt I normally experience when I'm not on vacation. No wonder I awake feeling calm, carefree, and thoroughly refreshed.

You don't have to be on vacation to enjoy a legitimate nap. It is said that John F. Kennedy actually undressed, turned down the sheets, and climbed into bed for daily catnaps. You might stretch out on the living room couch while dinner is in the oven. On a Sunday afternoon, crawl under the covers for an hour or so. When visiting your parents, try slipping off to your old bedroom or a spare room to catch 40 winks. Once when my daughter was house-sitting for us, she informed us she had the best snooze she's ever had while snuggled on a cushioned wicker sofa in our screened porch. "Going home" to snooze has the potential to induce the most comforting memories of a carefree childhood.

Napping allows a much-needed break from reality. No situation is so tough it can't be softened with a nap. Napping smoothes the ragged edges and mends the tattered places. Unlike sleeping, which we do because our physical bodies need rejuvenating, a nap restores the soul and lets creativity soar. With this innocent pleasure, hopes are repaired, wishes are rebuilt, and dreams are rekindled.

DELIGHT IN
GOD'S CREATURES

*If your dog or cat thinks you're
the most wonderful person in the world,
don't go looking for a second opinion!*

f you want unconditional love and guaranteed loyalty, try looking to your pets. Anyone who has been adopted by a pet knows that if you dote on them, they'll supply the steadfast devotion you could only hope for from a human. They don't criticize or find fault. They don't try to change us, but allow us to be ourselves. We can be as grumpy, whiny, or out of sorts as we want, and they'll still adore us. Our pets are truly agreeable friends, forgiving our shortcomings and licking away our tears. Because they are less judgmental than people, we can let down our guard when they are around.

Whether your pet has feet, fins, or feathers, it can offer you the unlimited supply of comfort that research has discovered can help you live a longer and healthier life. As I watch the bundle of purring fur contentedly sleeping under the lamp on my desk, I'm convinced that God had this innocent pleasure in mind when He created our loving companions.

Pets have a wonderful way of interrupting our cares. They bring us back down to earth and remind us to be lighthearted. By magnetizing our attention, they provide a break from negative thoughts that produce stress. There's nothing more amusing than watching a playful puppy frolic or a cat try to find its way out of a paper bag. Even the gentle undulations of tropical fish can have a calming effect. Those pets that love to be touched and held provide some added benefits. Rhythmically petting an animal can induce deep relaxation in us and can play a role in satisfying our need for close physical contact. It is as though we were the ones being caressed.

An elderly couple wrote to me, describing how their cat helped them endure a devastating personal crisis involving severe financial challenges and a serious illness. At times, they suffered bouts of despair and loneliness that nearly overwhelmed them, but laughing at the amusing antics of their playful kitten lifted their spirits. Stroking her soft, furry coat as she purred gave them a reason to smile. Their cat actually helped them to survive during their struggles.

My dad often stooped to stroke the family cat while fondly calling her a "time waster." To be sure, she was, but one he knew the value of. If you don't own a pet, consider walking a friend's dog, pet-sitting for a weekend through a private pound, or simply visiting the local zoo. In any case, nurture one of God's creatures along with yourself!

THE INSPIRING GARDEN

God Almighty first planted a garden.
And, indeed, it is the purest
of human pleasures.

FRANCIS BACON

This past spring, a friend shared with me that she had discovered an inspiring innocent pleasure in gardening, especially with roses. Interestingly, her favorite rose is a pale beauty named Pleasure.

When I contemplate pleasures and gardens in the same thought, I am instantly carried back to my favorite childhood book, *The Secret Garden* by Frances Hodgson Burnett. All the intense sensations I experienced then, although only in my mind—the sweet perfume of the flowers, the cool shade of the trees, the refreshing, fragrant rain showers—return to soothe and invigorate me once again.

The Secret Garden is a heartening story of the restoration of two forlorn and ill-tempered children—a frail, melancholy boy and a scrawny, cantankerous girl—brought together by misfortune. They discover an abandoned overgrown garden hidden inside old stone walls obscured by thick tangled vines. When they find the key to the heavy wooden door, they decide to visit the garden daily. Secretly they resurrect it, and, being fully immersed in nature, are themselves nurtured back to health and happiness.

Simply reminiscing about the story, I benefit once again as my senses are aroused by thoughts of this secluded haven with the winding garden trails, the pungent aroma of freshly turned earth, and the musty scent of moss-covered stepping stones. Engraved in my imagination are the sweet smell of spring blossoms, the brilliant hue of flowers in bloom, and the grandeur of aged sundials, majestic birdbaths, and stately walls draped in ivy. Merely imagining the splendor of it all gets my creativity surging, and I feel as though I must write a poem or compose a song.

To inspire means literally to "breathe into and infuse with life." Inspiring activities incite our passions, rouse us from inertia, enliven our senses, and restore our souls. Claude Monet once proclaimed, "I perhaps owe having become a painter to flowers." Reflections of a garden just may inspire you, too.

CREATE YOUR
GARDEN SANCTUARY

*I do not understand how
anyone can live without one small
place of enchantment to turn to.*

MARJORIE KINNAN RAWLINGS

ou may not be able to create an authentic "secret garden," but you can always choose one isolated spot to retreat to when you need a refuge from the phone, the fax, and the world. Yours could be a vine-covered trellis leading to a secluded niche, an arbor opening onto a shady nook, the sheltered haven of a backyard gazebo, or a private hideaway on a sunny balcony. Any little alcove will do if you can fit in a comfortable chair and a small table and go there when you are pining for the tranquillity of nature.

There is so much enchantment and pleasure to be found in gardening that it's been rightly called "horticultural therapy"— a healing journey for mind, body, and soul. Aside from the marvelous sense of fulfillment and satisfaction you experience, the exercise involved promotes physical and mental well-being. Even the weeding, cutting, and pruning have a way of releasing built-up tension. As you work with your plants, nurture them. Name them. Talk to them. Others may question your sanity, but you'll be so absorbed in the positive benefits, you won't even notice!

For me, the simple act of watering my gardens at the end of a full day of writing or lecturing is one of the most calming innocent pleasures I can experience. Like Marjorie Kinnan Rawlings, I don't know how people survive without one small place of grace and charm to retreat to!

A GARDEN ANYWHERE

*I look upon the pleasure which we take
in a garden as one of the most
innocent delights in human life.*

JOSEPH ADDISON

ot all of us have backyards suited for creating a
garden sanctuary. Don't despair if you live in an
apartment or have a small yard. Window boxes
or container gardens in tubs, urns, barrels, and baskets can
brighten a small space. Use pots in a variety of sizes to decorate
your patio or deck, or get some five-gallon buckets for growing
tomatoes, green onions, basil, and other summertime favorites.
Plant some fresh herbs in a kitchen planter box, and use the
surplus later to make potpourri or flavored vinegars and oils.
Herbs take up little space and can be grown all year round. The
sensational smell of an herb garden filled with oregano, basil,
thyme, parsley, rosemary, and dill will rejuvenate you every
time you pass by. Having fresh herbs available may also inspire
you to be more creative in your cooking.

If gardening truly isn't a possibility for you, seek out some
public parks or gardens in your area that you can retreat to
now and again. Watch local advertising for flower shows or
backyard garden tours. Pick up a bouquet at the market

(instead of waiting for someone to bring you flowers!) or buy a single orchid or rose from the florist. Arrange a few spring blossoms in some small colored glass bottles to put in a window or on your desk.

As an antidote for the winter blues, visit a local greenhouse, nursery, or garden center. Stroll through a fragrant arboretum or an especially delightful florist shop. Linger over the flowers, smell them, and get to know their names. Go to the library and check out garden picture books to browse through, and imagine yourself sitting somewhere surrounded by flowers. Cut out garden pictures from a landscaping or country living magazine, and make a collage that you can display in full view. Do a simple sketch or watercolor of your favorite flower whether or not you consider yourself an artist. There are many ways to appreciate flowers and plants. So abandon your daily tasks for a minute or two. Forsake your worries and cares. Wander into your garden sanctuary.

THE REFRESHING GARDEN

The green of the meadows, the scent of
the flowers, the shade of the trees
and the fragrant showers refresh
me and everything in its labors.

GONZALES DE BERCEO

For me, gardening was an unanticipated source of exhilaration. Shortly after I began exploring the value of practicing innocent pleasures, I planted my first backyard flower bed and discovered the invigorating joy of wandering into my personal sanctuary in the early morning stillness. When sunshine pours through tree branches as they sway in the morning breeze, shimmering patterns dance on the moist lawn. While leaves and petals are still heavy with dew, I sit quietly for a few moments in anticipation of the day ahead.

Today, the birdbath hosted two splashing visitors while a dozen or so butterflies fluttered nearby. As I delighted in the tranquillity of it all, I sensed that I was being miraculously transported into paradise. The surrounding color and beauty and abundance filled me with a great sense of contentment and serenity. I offered up a prayer of thanksgiving for this bit of heaven on earth, wondering if I had been allowed a taste of the Garden of Eden. Perhaps this divine allure of the garden was what the Persian poet, Sadi, referred to when he said, "A garden is a delight to the eye, and a solace to the soul; it soothes angry passions and produces that pleasure which is a foretaste of paradise."

When you're feeling overwhelmed by the pressures of time restraints and To Do lists, retreat to your garden. When you are plagued with stress, you'll find that petty annoyances and trivial irritations are subdued here. As you dig and plant and weed, dilemmas will seem to dissipate, and problems solve themselves. In the garden, it is nearly impossible to sense anything but pleasure!

REST IN A ROCKING CHAIR

Rest is the sweet sauce of labor.

PLUTARCH

A rocking chair is one of life's most enduring, all-natural, low-cost relaxants. After a time of fervent, passionate labor, nothing beats the soothing, innocent pleasure of a rocker to bring peace and tranquillity. The gentle rhythmic creaking of my cherished old rocker comforts me and lulls me into a serene, tranquil state. As I rock back and forth, wrapped in a cozy quilt and hidden away from the world, the cares of the day seem to float off into the distance much like balloons that have tugged long enough to free themselves at last from their restraints.

I associate so many warm memories with rocking chairs. As a child, I often crawled onto my grandma's bountiful, apron-clad lap as she rocked in her favorite chair. There I snuggled, either for the sheer comfort and delight of nestling with her, or to have a favorite bedtime story told yet one more time.

Then there's the rocker where I soothed my own sweet babies back to sleep after nursing them in the wee hours of the morning. What precious memories! When we moved from the house where I had rocked my children so often, the empty corner where the chair once sat saddened me, but I now have the pleasure of rocking my grandchildren in that same rocker in its new location.

The wicker rocking chair on the screened porch has its own special purpose. It's there that I can take a much-needed leisurely respite from my day's activities to sip iced tea and shut my eyes. In no time, I become enveloped in the soothing serenity of nature, calmed by a bird's serenade, hushed by the pleasant breezes all around, and pacified by the gentle to-and-fro motion of my chair. Even a few moments is enough to re-energize me for the balance of the day.

Find a rocking chair where you can sit and simply relax, allowing the pleasant repetition of the movement to soothe you. Let the rhythm wash away the cares of the day and lull you into memories of pleasant times gone by.

PART 5

INSTANT PLEASURES

WELCOME THE
WIND IN YOUR HAIR

*Thou wind! which art the unseen
similitude of God the Spirit,
His most sweet and mightiest sign.*

PHILIP BAILEY

hen was the last time you actually felt the wind blowing through your hair? Or would you rather bundle up and hunker down when someone opens the car windows, especially if your hair has just been styled and sprayed? I used to be known for perfect, wind-proof hairdos that would probably survive a hurricane; then I bought my first convertible. Now when I arrive to pick up the grand-children for some special outing, they all shout, "Here comes Grandma Sue with her top down!" Of course they're referring to the car, but it sure provides a good chuckle for everyone. These days, having my hair mussed is just about the last thing on my mind. The best part of owning a convertible is the inde-scribable sensation of the wind blowing wildly through my hair. Talk about a bad hair day! But I've learned to relax and enjoy the liberating sensation of pure windblown abandon-ment.

Whether you're on vacation in the Caribbean with breezes blowing steadily—every day is a bad hair day there—driving in the car with all the windows down, riding a motorcycle, or walking outside in a brisk breeze, simply relax and enjoy the freedom of having no boundaries and limits.

Seek out opportunities to feel wind blow through your hair. You can restyle your hairdo, but the sheer sense of liberation that comes with the wind can't be replicated. Embrace it with total abandon!

GO BAREFOOT

*No day is so difficult that it
can't be made easier by
taking off one's shoes and socks!*

ave you ever noticed how babies attempt to take
their shoes off at every opportunity? When my
children first had their tootsies packaged and
smothered in little white baby boots, they quickly learned how
to get out of them. They knew instinctively that feet were not
meant to be wrapped and suffocated. They yearned for the
freedom and joy of baring their chubby little toes once again,
and they did everything within their power to make that
happen.

Many of us learned to keep our feet properly shod to the
reverberating sound of our mothers saying "Where are your
shoes?" or "You're sure to get cut stepping on broken glass."
There were warnings of bees in the lawn and concern about
our feet getting cold. We were told to put on at least a pair of
bedroom slippers or socks, but always to wear something that
would ultimately render our feet concealed and disguised.

There's something deliciously frivolous about going barefoot. Stress and anxiety dissipate, and challenges are easier to

endure when our feet are free. Once we are without shoes, our entire mind-set changes. Bare feet invoke a relaxed outlook and an unbusinesslike manner. Enterprising endeavors and zealous undertakings fade into the distance. Intense competition with all its winning and achieving isn't nearly as crucial anymore. (Perhaps that's the reason why employees are usually required to wear shoes!) Walking around with our feet occasionally unclad and exposed is an innocent pleasure worth experiencing more often.

Can you remember the last time you went barefoot? Maybe you were strolling on a warm sandy beach or wiggling your toes in the freshly mown lawn at a backyard picnic. Perhaps it was the time when, as a child, you were making your way across a frigid creek. In any case, it's time to do it again. The textures of a nubby carpet, a plush rug, or the cool, moist grass beneath an unshod foot are invigorating and refreshing, helping to revive our nearly forgotten childhood. Be on the lookout for opportunities to experience the pleasure of going barefoot. Take off your shoes and socks just to dig your toes into the moist earth or splash in a puddle. Whatever experience you choose, be a child again, and revel in the sensation.

FIND WONDER
IN LITTLE THINGS

*You know you're old when
you've lost all your marvels.*

MERRY BROWNE

alph Waldo Emerson said that if the constellations appeared only once in a thousand years, it would be an exciting event indeed! But because they are there every night, we barely give them a second glance. One of the great tragedies of life is losing our sense of wonder. We know too much. We've tried everything and experienced all the thrills. We get so used to things that we no longer marvel at the simple miracles all around us.

Notice how children face life with a sense of awe and wonder. They see each day as a breathless voyage of discovery. Our granddaughter, Cassie, is a toddler who loves to spot an airplane in the sky. She'll wait forever with her head tilted high and tiny finger pointed to the skies if she thinks she hears an airplane in the distance. What jubilation she expresses when at last the plane comes into view! Her entire body responds as she squeals with delight, pointing out this spectacle to anyone who will look.

Some of us get so familiar with even the miraculous that we lose our reverence. We engage in oblivious chatter about everything from other people's attitudes to our future dreams and plans, yet few things can cause us to stand and gaze in open-mouthed wonder. We meander through life distracted by the everyday nature of tasks and duties, overlooking the beauty of a wildflower springing up along a path, the brilliant colors in autumn leaves, the subtle radiance of a rainbow, or the resplendent beauty of a sunset.

Have you lost all your marvels? Maybe you've just become too accustomed to your surroundings. Make the effort to stop and pet the gleeful puppy who comes bouncing up to greet you or to watch a spirited horse playfully circling a corral. Enjoy a quietly sinking sun or return a friendly smile. Begin to take note of little joys here and there, and you will soon see splendor in the ordinary. As John Burroughs commented, "I still find each day too short for all the thoughts I want to think, all the walks I want to take, all the books I want to read, and all the friends I want to see. The longer I live, the more my mind dwells upon the beauty and wonder of the world."

WATER ON THE INSIDE

Water is the only drink
for a wise man.

HENRY DAVID THOREAU

hen it comes to increasing energy levels, maintaining weight, and improving general health, few things are as helpful as water. Let pure water do wonders for you. When thirst signals that your body is low on water, are you tempted to go for coffee, tea, or cola? The caffeine in these beverages has a dehydrating effect, which defeats the purpose. Instead, drink a glass of water first, and then enjoy a cup of herbal tea or juice if you still want it. If you have water each time your body calls out for a drink, you won't need nearly as much of the other drinks you've been having during the day.

Because I drink water often, I thought I consumed at least my daily quota of eight glasses. But when I measured it to be sure, I found that I had been drinking only four to five eight-ounce glasses in a day. Now to be sure I get my full eight or more glasses, I keep a stack of eight pennies close by, transferring one to a new pile each time I finish a glass of water.

Watching the stack grow encourages me to keep going until I've reached or surpassed my quota.

Now I always keep a glass of water near me in clear view. When it is empty, I refill it. That way it's more convenient than other drinks that I might be tempted to choose. When I'm away from my home or office or in my car, I carry bottled water.

Water is the great purifier of life—without and within. It acts as a magnet in attracting impurities and flushing out wastes, transports oxygen and nutrients through the blood, provides an additional source of minerals, and aids in weight loss. If you haven't been drinking eight or more glasses a day, develop the habit, and you'll be surprised at how quickly your natural thirst returns. Wonderful, miraculous water—truly an innocent pleasure!

TAKE A STROLL

*When we stroll, we give passionate attention
to the details around us and to our lives.*

trolling is fast becoming a lost art. Strolling is not the same as walking. When I think of taking a walk, which I love to do, my mind instantly conjures images of a rigorous fitness regimen and the desire to get in shape. But strolling is different. It is a slow-paced saunter that allows you to ramble aimlessly and roam freely without any time constraints. To stroll is to meander, pause, and explore—things we can't do when we're on a fitness mission.

Even saying the word "stroll" is calming to me. It's a word we don't hear often enough in our present-day vocabulary. In today's fast-paced world, strolling sounds like something our grandparents did on a Sunday afternoon in the park. When I was a child, people took evening strolls through the neighborhood, stopping to chat once in a while with another stroller or with the next-door neighbor who was sipping an after-dinner coffee on the veranda. Back then, it seems, there was definitely an art to strolling!

When you're lacking peace or feeling down in your spirit and need a fresh touch of the divine in life, take a stroll. It may be around the block or simply out to the mailbox. When you stroll, deliberately quiet your mind, slow your breathing, loosen your joints, and let your muscles go slack. As you wander with a leisurely and unhurried stride, heading nowhere in particular, observe the world around you. Become aware of your surroundings, and contemplate the exquisite pictures God paints on the canvas of the world. Consider the scents, sounds, and textures of nature, the many shades of green in shrubs and trees, an unusual bird's nest, or two squirrels enjoying a game of tag. Notice a grandmother pushing a stroller and the child who's sleeping peacefully, or someone napping on a park bench. Say hello to children selling lemonade at a makeshift stand, and make sure you stop and buy some!

Taking a stroll means slowing down and perhaps reviving the long-forgotten comforts of neighborhood companionship. When we stroll, we often gain new insights into who we are, where we're headed, and how we'll get there. Decide to take a stroll and allow God to nourish your soul as you meander along.

ABANDON MODERN TECHNOLOGY FOR A DAY

The world is too much with us.

WILLIAM WORDSWORTH

My friend's grandmother, who used to complain, "You don't write, call, or visit nearly enough," now says, "You never fax or e-mail!" The modern conveniences of quick communication pervade our society. But do they always enhance our quality of life? Some people lament the grip of technology on our lives. The poet Mr. Wordsworth might have felt that way two hundred years ago! Today, more than ever, we all need an occasional break from the phone, pager, fax, and computer. Those things can help us feel connected, but sometimes we need to deliberately break away from them to seek a few tranquil moments. Only when we quiet the clamor of the outside world can we hear the whisper of God's voice giving us new direction.

Recently, I accidentally left my cellular phone behind for a weekend. I don't use it very often, so I didn't think I'd miss it. I was wrong! I felt positively lost without it. While running errands, I wondered who might be thinking I was rude by not getting back to them. Wasn't I obligated to retrieve messages and return calls? Finally, when I accepted my dilemma, I experienced a euphoric sense of freedom. After all, I knew I had a legitimate excuse for not returning calls that day, and it started me thinking about the incredible pleasure of being free from the paraphernalia of modern technology for a day or two.

Every now and then, plan your escape. Experience one full day without e-mail. Turn off the TV for a while. Don't answer the phone. (Remember when taking it off the hook was enough? That doesn't work anymore; now you must turn the sound off.) By not answering, you are accepting responsibility for your peace of mind. Turn off your radio and tape player too, especially while you're driving. Forget the Walkman when you're exercising or jogging. Don't wear your watch, and notice how liberated you feel with no concept of time passing you by.

Noisy beepers, machines, and timers ring or buzz incessantly and steadily remind us that someone is waiting for our attention. Our world has a sense of emergency about it. I appreciate the words of historian James Truslow Adams: "Perhaps it would be a good idea someday, fantastic as it sounds, to muffle every telephone, quiet every motor, and stop all activity—just to give people a chance to ponder and reflect on what life is all about, why they are living, and what they really want." Experiment with this innocent pleasure. You may find it easier to escape once in a while than you thought possible!

WHEREVER YOU ARE, BE THERE

Right now a moment of time is fleeting by!
Capture its reality...become that moment.

PAUL CÉZANNE

To be here now is an innocent pleasure that has been transforming my life. Simply put, it means to embrace a moment in time and seize the very essence of it. How often we are somewhere in body, but somewhere else in our thoughts!

The other morning as I was walking along the beach, I found myself wishing I could share the glorious sunlight glistening on the water, the brilliant blue sky, and the enormous fluffy clouds with my husband, my daughters, or our grandchildren. My self-talk became, "If only they were here with me, this morning's walk would be perfect." We fall into a trap: believing that something else has to take place before we can truly be in the moment and enjoy it for what it is. I had to remind myself, *It is a perfect day simply because I am here and it is now.*

Learning to be where you are is one of the most pleasurable ways to focus a busy mind and live fully. The next time you're at the grocery store, concentrate on the amazing variety of apples and lettuces, an egg's polished surface, the extra ingredient that turns dinner into a feast. If your mind drifts off and you begin to think about the project that is overdue, the fundraiser you're in charge of, the extra ten pounds you can't seem to drop, or the stack of files on your messy desk, gently bring it back. Be mindful of what you are doing and revel in each moment. As Thomas Merton put it, "The meaning of life is found in being present in full awareness."

Choose to Be Here Now. Write the initials BHN in a bold black marker on an index card and post it where you can see it often. Life is not like your VCR—there is no pause, stop, or rewind. A moment cannot be recaptured, relived, or improved upon. There may never be another day so rich in opportunities and possibilities as today. Right now a moment of time is passing by. Seize it! Become the moment. As H.L. Mencken reminded us, "We are here and it is now."

TAKE TIME
TO REMINISCE

When Time, who steals our years away,
Shall steal our pleasures too,
The mem'ry of the past will stay,
And half our joys renew.

THOMAS MOORE

Time is fleeting, but there is one place where time can stand still: our memories. There is always time enough for the innocent pleasure of reminiscing, but only if we purpose in our hearts to stop and reflect for a moment.

What's happening in your life today has a lot to do with people and events from the past. Embrace the wisdom and beauty of those experiences by taking a few moments to ponder them. While it's true that most days it's enough to simply keep up with building new memories for ourselves and our families, reminiscing allows us to taste a delicious slice of our life once again.

Isn't it gratifying to spend time with others who have similar memories? Telling stories from the past is one of the things I enjoy most about getting together with family and friends. Children especially love to hear stories of when they were small. They want you to tell them over and over again, and they never tire of hearing them.

Recall precious moments from childhood and enjoy being young again—the day you made the perfect snow angel or blew a huge, shimmering, rainbow-colored bubble and miraculously caught it on your wand. Savor in your memory the time you rode a merry-go-round, built sand castles at the beach, or romped in autumn leaves. Reflect upon a day when you felt special—a momentous birthday, your wedding day, or graduation. Celebrate once again those past achievements—winning an award, accepting a trophy, or performing in a piano concert or dance recital. Think about the special people, pets, family times, and vacations that added to your life. Remember someone who is no longer with you, either due to distance or death. Recalling the ways someone touched your life and focusing on how it has changed you for the better makes you grateful.

We've all experienced events worth celebrating. Don't lose those memories in the push to move on to future plans and events. Permit yourself to relive happy moments, and revel in them once again.

ADD A LITTLE BUFFOONERY TO YOUR LIFE

A little nonsense now and then
is relished by the wisest men.

ROALD DAHL,
Willy Wonka

veryone should indulge in a little malarkey now and again. My friend tells me her father leaves humorous messages or comical drawings on a few squares of toilet paper to amuse the next visitor! Another good friend called me one morning on a whim to ask if I'd like to go to a nearby lakeside park to ride the antique merry-go-round and then get an ice-cream cone. An exuberant young mom I once met on a plane told me she wears different hats during the day—a chauffeur's cap while carting the kids around, a chef's stovepipe when fixing a meal—even if it's wieners and beans—and a bandanna, beret, or beanie when mowing the lawn. Even if her family thinks she's wacky, I'm sure they benefit from her happy-go-lucky, playful spirit.

Think of the people you know who honor the child within. Children have the gift of whimsical impulsiveness and can totally abandon themselves to sudden inspiration. I don't mean to suggest that we act childish, but rather, childlike. There is a big difference.

Perhaps if we could get lost in the pleasure of buffoonery more often, we'd be less concerned about others' opinions of us. Try this. Think about what people least expect of you, and then do it! Indulge in the perfect fantasy. What if you wore white leather boots, a huge belt buckle, and a cowboy hat to your next family event? How about turning a somersault on the front lawn just as company arrives or serving animal crackers and chocolate pudding for dessert? Color your hair burgundy with one of the new wash-out sprays you can pick up at a beauty supply shop. If you're stuck in traffic, blow bubbles out the window and wear funny glasses or a red clown nose.

Imagine how your life would be different if you were to devote an entire day to some lighthearted spontaneity and silliness! All Fools' Day—April 1—has always been accepted as a day for playing pranks and all sorts of trickery, but it can also be a good reminder to do something amusing more than once a year. When you find yourself taking life too seriously or you're about to snap someone's head off, do something ludicrous and outlandish. Be absurd and preposterous. It will help you gain the relief and perspective you may desperately need. I can't promise it works every time, but if it works once, it's worth the effort. And you'll enjoy a few laughs along the way.

MAKE YOUR OWN MUSIC

When troubles come, go at them with songs;
when griefs arise, sing them down;
lift the voice of praise against cares.

HENRY WARD BEECHER

rederick Delius called music an "outburst of the soul." The other day I listened to big band music while baking some apple cinnamon muffins and caught myself humming along to the melody. As my humming turned to singing, it brought back memories of the gatherings my parents often had in our home where everyone crowded around to sing while Dad belted out their favorites on the piano. I wonder if we have forgotten how to sing along. My mother always sang along with the radio as she prepared dinner, ironed, frosted a cake, or dusted furniture.

People used to sing while they worked, knowing that "little by little the time goes by; short if you sing, long if you sigh." If they weren't singing or humming, they were whistling, even while walking down the street. Although singing in the streets could be taken as a sign of mental imbalance or drunkenness, whistling was acceptable. It brightened the day and made a dark night a lot less scary. Apparently technology has taken care of all that, and now those who like a tune to lighten their load just plug into a headset, as though making music were best left to those who earn a living at it.

Whether singing, whistling, or clapping your hands, you are making music. One of my favorite sounds is that of my husband whistling as he comes through the back door each evening after work. What a joyful talent he has! As a non-whistler, I can't imagine why anyone would hold back such a gift. My father, who was also a jubilant whistler, often commented that we don't always whistle when we're happy, but we'll always be happy if we whistle!

Psychologists tell us that making music is good for the mind, the body, and the spirit. After all, you can't stay angry with someone while you're singing. And it's hard to feel lonely or dreary on a rainy day if you're whistling. Maybe you can't carry a tune in a bucket, and you wouldn't dare sing out loud in public, but you can sing along with the radio or a tape. You can sing in the shower or alone in your car. Go ahead and sing and hum and whistle. Do it out loud. Do it with passion! See how making music changes your situation. See how it changes you!

DANCE BY YOURSELF!

Let them praise His name in the dance.

PSALM 149:3

fter playing a wonderful concert in a magnificent candlelit amphitheater, a renowned violinist and his orchestra made a medley of familiar waltzes their grand finale. One couple after another rose to dance to the "Skaters' Waltz," the "Blue Danube," and several other favorites. I will never forget their silhouettes gracefully twirling up and down the aisles. With full-skirted evening gowns rustling and hair flowing freely they danced the evening away in total abandon. I kept thinking of how liberating it must have been for them.

Perhaps someone has told you—or you have convinced yourself—that you are too heavy, too awkward, or too old to dance. If so, you may shy away from this innocent pleasure. Heaven forbid that anyone should spot *you* dancing in a concert hall! Yet when you're all alone, you can dance without worrying about anyone seeing you. Because you make the rules, you can enjoy dancing regardless of your size, dexterity, or age.

Look for opportunities to dance. When you're gardening, skip between the flower beds or leap through the lawn sprinkler! Put on some big band tunes and boogie as you prepare breakfast, or dance in the moonlight to your favorite classical pieces. Tune the radio to an oldies station, kick off your shoes, and have a sock hop in your living room. Close the drapes, shut yourself away, and make sure you have on comfortable clothing that allows for movement. At first you may feel silly swaying, jumping, jiggling, and twirling. Do it anyway. Give yourself time to feel comfortable with the rhythmic movement of your own body. Experiment with various moves. Some will feel better to you than others. Go with those that seem natural. Dance until you lose sight of yourself. Dance with abandon, your heart focused on giving thanks to God for the freedom you're experiencing, your body expressing the feelings you have deep within.

In a recent popular flick, a female star had flashbacks to times she and her mother would twirl together, round and round the room, just for fun. Why not find a large space of your own, play wild music, spread your arms wide, and whirl around in circles? Then, just keep moving, faster and faster, casting all your cares, worries, and frustrations heavenward. Remember, no one is watching. This is just between you and God!

REJOICE IN THE
WONDERS OF WATER

*One of the most soothing sounds of nature
is the laughter of falling water.*

JEFF COX

A soak in a hot spring or sulfur bath to the sound of a babbling brook, or the view while sitting at the water's edge gazing across the vast expanse—the sights and sounds of running water are naturally therapeutic and restore your sense of well-being. Thundershowers in summertime dancing on your roof, a waterfall splashing in the woods, a fountain in the park—they all have a rejuvenating effect. The fine spray at the seashore touches your skin, and you breathe it in. Waves bounce off the rocky beach or slap up against the shore, and their sound soothes and comforts you. Water is nature's most readily available invigorator, always restoring and refreshing.

Who doesn't love vacationing near water? A friend who recently took a seashore vacation reported that all of the rooms in her hotel faced the water. After all, who wants to gaze out at land, even at landscaped gardens, if you could watch the pounding surf instead?

There's a screened-in porch facing the woods at the back of our house. I love to sit in my wicker rocking chair during warm summer showers, surrounded by the balmy mist and the rain beating a gentle rhythm on the roof. A magical tranquillity takes over. As I watch the magnificence of nature unleashed, cares are washed away. Within a few minutes I am cleansed, and I feel a wonderful sensation of well-being.

Whether soaking or swimming in it, listening to it, or merely observing it, water is one of nature's most innocent pleasures, drawing us back to the proverbial peace of the womb, encouraging us to stay in touch with our earliest source of comfort and contentment.

PART 6

TURNING THE PAGES

FAMILY AND FRIENDS IN 8 X 10S:

Enjoy the Magic of Photographs

Photographs...capture a moment that people cannot always see.

HENRY CALLAHAN

One of my photo albums captures memories of my sisters' annual weekend retreat. The five of us—no husbands, no kids—gather once a year, commuting from across North America, to spend a few days together reconnecting and catching up. Mostly it's a time of laughter and tears, good food, long talks, sleepless nights, and outrageous silliness. Our photographs document the entire event. They capture the moments and keep the memories alive. My sisters all agree that by simply looking at the pictures, we can return in an instant to the time, the place, and the intensity of the feelings we experienced.

Another of my albums displays snapshots of our grandchildren, first as newborns, then every subsequent month for their first year, and each year thereafter on their birthdays. Of course, this collection is a never-ending work in progress! Still other albums have themes such as children, young and old, frolicking in huge piles of fragrant autumn leaves in our front yard, or various family members blowing out candles on birthday cakes. Another shows some of the unique and often hilarious road signs we have noticed on our travels over the years.

Through the magic of photographs, I can relive precious moments any time I choose. Miraculously, I am transported back in time to savor the aromas, flavors, sounds, and textures associated with the event as it resonates in my imagination.

Photos are innocent pleasures that capture memories and evoke a medley of emotional responses. They have the unique ability to stop time and stir feelings. They chronicle our history and provide a visual account of our most meaningful experiences. They can act as a tremendous resource when we need comfort, when our spirits need reviving, and when our lives need a touch of enchantment or inspiration. Wouldn't it be nice if you could actually go back and relive your favorite memories? Reminiscing with your photographs is the next best thing to doing just that.

ESCAPE IN A GOOD BOOK

A book is a garden, an orchard,
a storehouse, a party, a company by the way,
a counselor, a multitude of counselors.

HENRY WARD BEECHER

ow I love books! They have always been a refuge for me, a place of solitude and seclusion, a wellspring of relaxation, recreation, and restoration. On those rare occasions when I find myself without a book close by, I actually feel deprived. Occasionally I've been reduced to reading cereal packages at the breakfast table or road signs from the passenger seat of the car for lack of proper reading material. But read I must, and I find books the most comforting of companions.

My love of books began when I was a child. My parents placed large piles of reading material at the foot of my bed each night as they "tucked me in." The idea was to keep me occupied at the crack of dawn when I woke up before the rest of the family, because no one wanted to be disturbed that early. Since then, books have been a source of inspiration and strength, faithful teachers helping to build and shape my life. My favorite books have become like friends, filling in what might otherwise be lonely moments. As Elizabeth Barrett Browning penned, "No man can be called friendless when he has God and the companionship of good books."

Take a break from your daily challenges and worries. Escape into the familiar world of a well-known book, or delve into one you've never read. Through books, you can embark on a spine-tingling safari, set sail on a tempestuous ocean voyage, or be part of a perilous Arctic expedition. Any time you choose, you can journey through the continents or travel through time. You might be thrown into the middle of an ominous mystery or allowed the privilege of braving someone else's life experiences through an autobiography. Whether you're reading something that is hilarious and wildly amusing or contemplative and reflective, books are innocent pleasures that bring enjoyment to your day-to-day life. Have you read any good books lately? I hope so, because that old adage may be true—the one who does not read is no better off than the one who cannot read.

SURROUND YOURSELF
WITH BOOKS

*When we are collecting books,
we are collecting happiness.*

VINCENT STARRETT

For me, the sight, scent, and texture of books are comforting and full of promise. I like to have a good selection in every room—on bookshelves, in wicker baskets, stacked on the floor next to my favorite easy chair, piled on the nightstand. I have books in my car, my briefcase, and my handbag. By placing books anywhere I regularly find myself, I am continually immersed in their aura of contentment and inspiration, and reading material is always readily available when the mood strikes or time allows.

To prime the well of my imagination when I am preparing to write, I sit surrounded by my cherished collection of well-worn books, armed with a new spiral notebook and my favorite pen. With a beautiful CD of classical melodies playing in the background, a candle lit nearby, and a fresh pot of hot tea served up in my favorite china cup, my creative juices soon begin to flow. Before long, I am writing furiously, as though divinely guided. Once I have written my longhand notes, I go to my office and start the editing process on the computer.

Dependably, books provide the spark that ignites my inspiration.

The public library has its own allure. The library card has been called the single greatest bargain in the world today, yet I was astounded when I heard results of a study reporting that less than 3 percent of those who have one actually use it. Why not recapture the joy of wandering through the library? Breathe in the atmosphere. Stay as long as you want. While you're there, choose some books you typically would not choose, whether they be fiction, real-life adventures, or biographies— whatever would be a break away from the norm for you. As Sir Richard Steele reminded us, "Reading is to the mind what exercise is to the body."

BUILD YOUR PERSONAL LIBRARY

When I get a little money, I buy books;
if any is left, I buy food and clothes.

DESIDERIUS ERASMUS

There's an old adage that says you can tell a lot about a person by his library. John Kieran admitted, "I am a part of all I have read." Knowing how true both statements are, over the years I have carefully built my own library, acquiring hundreds of books that have proved to be invaluable sources of information, inspiration, and insight. The right books can provide me with courage to move forward and confirmation that I am headed in the right direction. They offer sound advice and affirm what we intuitively know to be true. Books explain our miracles and help to bring about new ones. Christopher Morley said, "When you sell a man a book, you don't just sell him twelve ounces of paper and ink and glue— you sell him a whole new life." It's true; many lives have been transformed after reading just one book.

My library is a hodgepodge of fact and fiction, a conglomeration of books on personal discovery and spiritual growth, historical novels, adventure stories, and how-to books on every topic imaginable. Others contain enlightening quotes, whimsical cartoons, or eloquent poetry. I have books filled with pictures of charming country inns I hope to visit and mouth-watering recipes I plan to try. My shelves are brimming with a wide selection of tantalizing titles.

If you need encouragement or a new outlook, try spending an afternoon or evening browsing through a bookstore. Check out different shops until you find one that feels good, and then visit it often. When you go, leave your watch at home. Inhale the clean smell of crisp, new pages. Enjoy the luxury of moving from section to section at your leisure, tasting some books, digesting others.

Whenever I indulge myself this way, I always leave with a new "friend" or two to add to my collection. When my husband sees me coming through the front door laden with bags of books, he reminds me of the bumper sticker he saw recently that says "So many books, so little time!" My sentiments exactly.

LOSE YOURSELF IN CHILDREN'S BOOKS

A truly great book should be read
in youth, again in maturity
and once more in old age....

ROBERTSON DAVIES

There's nothing childish about reading a children's book. Yes, *Anne of Green Gables* was written for young girls, but you'll find a whole new story in its pages as an adult. When Anne dyes her hair green or accidentally gets her friend tipsy on raspberry cordial, your sympathy will now lie as much with the parents as with Anne. And in *Peter Pan*, you'll chuckle at your own unbending rules when Wendy won't let the children swim from the rock until they've rested a full half-hour after lunch, even though Captain Hook is fast approaching.

What were your favorites as a child? Search them out again. They'll bring back glimpses of who you were and what sparked your imagination. A friend of mine relishes the fact that her son loves the same books as she did, giving her the chance to read aloud *The Hobbit, Silver Chief,* and *The Sword in the Stone.*

Use books to connect with the children you know. A woman who works with foster children couldn't seem to relate to a very sullen little boy. One night, though, she brought along a copy of Louis Sacher's *Holes,* a recent Newbery Award book. "You're reading that?" he said. When she admitted she'd barely started it, he said, "Well, finish it before you come again, and we can talk about it." And they did!

Visit the children's section of your library for a fresh perspective on the joys of reading. The books there faithfully call us to reconnect with the awe and wonder of the reading days of our childhood. Do you remember visiting the library, doing research for school assignments or science fair projects, or taking out books for vacation or a long weekend? Experience again the simplicity, enchantment, and expectancy books brought to you as a child.

GIVE POETRY A CHANCE!

Poetry is the music of thought,
conveyed to us in the music of language.

PAUL CHATFIELD

f you're like me, you have some frightful memories of trying to analyze poems in English class. Although I did enjoy the occasional poem, I often felt intimidated and viewed poetry as an art that only the highly educated could appreciate. Yet poets tell us they see poetry as genuine, sincere, and personal. They claim it has the ability to induce a sense of tranquillity and composure. In fact today, in fields as diverse as dentistry and mental health, poetry is often used to help people relax and recover.

One psychiatrist suggested to patients who had trouble sleeping or were anxious or depressed, "Instead of aspirin, take two poems." Poetry acts as a healing remedy that soothes and restores, for as we study the words of a poem, we see that our experiences are universal. Someone, even if it's a long-dead English poet, understands what we are encountering! Reflecting on the turbulence inside us makes the intangible tangible, and gives us hope.

Although poetry doesn't always rhyme, it does have a rhythm, and it is that rhythm that gives it a balancing effect. It seems the poems we like best are the ones whose rhythms closely match our own body rhythms, restoring balance to our moods.

To begin experiencing this innocent pleasure, make poetry more accessible by listening to a tape or attending a good reading. Visit the library and select the works of a few poets to bring home and explore—try Henry Wadsworth Longfellow, Emily Dickinson, John Keats, Robert Louis Stevenson, Elizabeth Barrett Browning, Walt Whitman, or Oliver Wendell Holmes as a start. Read a poem each day. Ponder a few lines before going to bed. Meditate on the words and emotions of these poets to open up your own thoughts and feelings.

You may even want to explore writing poetry. Free from the restraint of perfectly formed sentences, poetry allows for freedom of expression through colorful phrases and random passages. Poetry is not really that mysterious. As someone once wisely expressed, it is the grouping of words, phrases, and ideas that have always loved each other but have never gotten into that combination before!

JOURNAL
YOUR THOUGHTS

To put our feelings into words—and
to later read our own words—
is a healing experience.

ournaling is one innocent pleasure that's been instrumental in taking my scarcely manageable lifestyle to a place of harmony and grace. Writing my thoughts enables me to find majesty in the mundane, divine in the dreary, splendor in the sorrows, and bliss in the burdens. It brings me to an awareness of the endless stream of blessings I encounter each day. Through journaling, I discover that every event in my life is significant enough to become cause for personal reflection and has the potential to be a source of revelation—the hurts, heartaches, disappointments, deadlines, bad hair days, the pan of sticky buns flipped upside down on the kitchen floor, car repairs, unexpected bills, a teenager's bedroom, and the monthly screaming meemies. Journaling has given me the divine awareness that my life can be a daily form of worship to my Creator. Most of us have more harried moments in our lives than tranquil ones; making journal entries helps to quiet the inner turmoil so we can begin to experience the symmetry, beauty, and harmony all around us.

Journaling has been described as a safety valve for the emotions, a device for clarifying our thoughts and working out solutions, a way to reflect on our faith, a spiritual growth encounter, a safe spot to list our prayers, and a method of recording our hopes, dreams, and life experiences. It's also a place to capture new ideas rather than lose those fleeting insights that bring momentary wisdom and perceptiveness. Henry David Thoreau expressed, "My journal is that of me which would else spill over and run to waste." More than anything, a journal is the soul made visible. Journaling crystallizes our thinking. With something tangible to examine, we are then better equipped to decipher hidden messages and sort out when to act, when to reflect, and when to release.

Journaling as a spiritual discipline has been in existence for centuries. You are a spiritual being that happens to live in a body; journaling is an invaluable means of connecting with the divine Spirit who is the very source of peace, joy, and heavenly direction. With your journal open and pen in hand, there is an expectancy, a readiness to hear what God is whispering into your heart. Cultivate the journal habit. Record your feelings, observations, and insights regularly. Journaling is a dynamic experience that draws from your past but makes an incredible impact on your future.

SHARE THE STORY
OF A LIFETIME

*Experiences of the moment
are tomorrow's memories.*

As you live each day, you are creating a unique work of art. Why not document your masterpiece as it unfolds? A great place to begin is to record some of your best-loved memories, perhaps as a gift for your family. To help get you going, write down your heartfelt responses to these ideas:

- Who gave you your name, and did you have a nickname?

- What was your favorite childhood pastime? Dessert? Toy? Author? Sport? School subject?

- Describe your first pet, job, date, valentine, school concert, birthday party, ball game, or fair.

- How did you and your family celebrate special holidays, and where did you go on vacations?

- Who were your best friends in school, and what did you do together?

- Tell one special memory about each of your brothers and sisters.

- What was the best gift you ever received, and who was it from? What is your most treasured possession?

- What chores were you expected to do around the house while you were growing up?

- What were some of your favorite family recipes?

- Did you have pets, and if so, what funny things did they do?

- Did your family ever endure a tragedy? How did it affect you?

- What were some of your youthful goals you've achieved or important lessons you've learned?

- Name one person who influenced your life profoundly.

- What word best describes your life and why?

Give as many details as possible, including scents, sounds, textures, flavors, and colors, to evoke a strong emotional response in your reader. Browse through photos to stimulate your senses. You may even want to include some snapshots in your finished work.

Design a cover with a picture of yourself or a collage of photographs, words, or meaningful images cut from magazines, overlapped and glued on heavy paper. Then have the whole page laminated. Check out how inexpensive it is to have your autobiography bound at an office supply store. Sharing your story is an innocent pleasure that can give your loved ones a sense of what family is all about—a feeling of belonging and connection, however far apart you are.

ALTERNATIVE JOURNALS

*Those who enter the gates of heaven
are not beings who have no passions or
have curbed the passions, but those who
have cultivated an understanding of them.*

WILLIAM BLAKE

Your daybook of thoughts and inspiration—the written daily dialogue that records your passions and pet peeves, dreams and disappointments—is one way to keep a journal. But there are other unique ways.

For example, over the years some of my favorite books—dog-eared and personalized with comments or dates jotted in the margins—have also become my journals. Those underlined or highlighted passages are clues about my deepest thoughts, either for my own introspection or for anyone who might someday flip through its pages. Just think of it—each time you mark a book to emphasize a point, you are in essence chronicling a portion of yourself. As I leaf through the many treasured volumes in my library that I've acquired from family members or friends, some who have passed on, I feel privileged to have a brief glimpse into their most intimate musings through their thoughtfully placed asterisks or check marks. The underscored sections and circled words reveal so much about the person who penned them.

Similarly, my grandmother's cookbooks and my mother's handwritten recipe cards leave a cherished legacy of their own. Enhanced with notations letting me know how popular this one was with company or how that one should be served with a special sauce ("see recipe on back of card"), they trigger memories of special people, the old kitchen table, and all the meals that were served there. Even the stains splattered on the paper remind me that as I work in my kitchen today, I am surrounded by a generation of cooks—their advice, their menus, their wisdom.

A visual journal is an intriguing way to unveil your hidden self. Artist's sketchbooks or bound blank books from an office supply store work well. Fill them with illustrations and sketches representing your dreams, images of health, fitness, decorating or landscaping, and symbols of comfort. With a stack of magazines, travel brochures, gardening catalogs, photographs, and greeting cards, plus scissors, a glue stick, and some colored markers, illustrate your life and dreams in expressive collages. Assemble your pictures at random on the pages and create beautiful images that spark your imagination. Then, on those days when you're feeling overwhelmed with responsibilities and obligations, relax and browse through each one. Reminding yourself of dreams worth working on is one way to make them come true.

LEAVE A PRECIOUS LEGACY

*In our family, an experience
was not finished, not truly
experienced, unless written down
or shared with another.*

ANNE MORROW LINDBERGH

During my grandmother's last few weeks with us, our family "interviewed" her about growing up on the farm, school days, church activities, how she met Grandpa, and who taught her to play the piano. Yes, we knew that she taught piano for most of her adult life, but there was so much more we didn't know. For instance, as a young woman she had played in a band on live radio every Friday evening! I'm so thankful we had that wonderful opportunity to hear her tell about her life. Sadly, there is still so much more we'll never know, but at least she is still with us through her colorful stories.

To capture these stories, turn a family gathering into a story night. Ask each person to share what they remember about a grandparent, a vacation, the old neighborhood, the schools you attended, the teachers you had. One family learned that their father, now a stodgy old banker, had scaled the steeple of his college's "Old Main" to steal the bell clapper, leaving the bell silent for graduation day! The brothers found out why their mother had allowed them to keep their garter snake in a cage right on the kitchen table ("If you had a snake in your house, wouldn't you want it right where you could keep an eye on it?").

If no one wants to take notes, record the evening on audio or video tape. Stories are powerful. If a picture is worth a thousand words, then a story is worth a million. When children, grandchildren, and future generations hear family stories, they see how they fit in, both at home and in the world. Tales of their heritage will create vivid, indelible images imprinted on their minds and lives for years to come.

PART 7

FAMILY PLEASURES

STRENGTHEN FAMILY TIES

Call it a clan, call it a network,
call it a tribe, call it a family.
Whatever you call it, whoever
you are, you need one.

JANE HOWARD

ince the beginning of time, people have lived in families. In some tribal medicine, a principal part of healing involved bringing the whole clan together to work things through. When someone was sick, the ancient healers would ask, "What is happening in this family that makes one of its branches ill?" The influence of the family was recognized and highly regarded. If people felt supported and loved, the immune system seemed to function better and healing was accelerated.

Loving family relationships are the best defense we can have against the challenges of the world. From tribes to clans, families over the years have eased our tensions, strengthened belief in our own abilities, helped ward off illness, and relieved anxiety, even though in some cases it might seem as if they cause as much as they heal!

Modern living puts an enormous strain on family harmony. Often today's families are so fragmented and busy that they communicate with each other only through notes on the kitchen counter. (Sitting in the same room glued to the TV set is a false togetherness unless the show was carefully chosen to yield discussion or reminiscences.) By showing a willingness to spend time together and an appreciation for each other, we can begin to heal our families. Children who are connected to a huge clan know they are thought of, cared about, and loved by a wide circle of people they are related to.

My family is always on the lookout for a chance to spend time with each other. Any event can become a reason for another gathering, from birthdays and anniversaries to holidays, engagements, new jobs, and new babies. If someone is going to be in town on a business trip, we'll be sure to meet. When one family member returns from a vacation, another arranges a party.

For years, the five girls in my family have met for a special sisters' weekend once a year. Naturally, it takes a commitment of time, effort, and money, and it isn't always convenient for everyone, but we've taken it seriously. As a result, we've formed a bond that can surpass the normal conflicts and differences families must deal with. I can relate to Lady Mary Wortley Montague when she said, "There can be no situation in life in which the conversation of my dear sister will not administer some comfort to me." Now I know why God designed the family in the beginning!

CELEBRATE
A TRADITION

How, but in custom and ceremony,
are innocence and beauty born?

WILLIAM BUTLER YEATS

One of our most delightful family traditions is an innocent pleasure we call Orange Popsicle Day. It began just days before the birth of my first daughter one early spring when our frosty winter weather changed to a sudden tropical heat wave that sent people scrambling to find cool clothing. Since my pregnancy was to be over before warm weather arrived, my maternity wardrobe consisted of woolly, winter outfits. Now, with my neighbors in shorts and bathing suits, I felt more uncomfortable than ever, and for some reason, I craved a Popsicle—specifically an *orange* Popsicle! So off I sauntered to the corner store to buy my icy treat. Satisfying my craving worked wonders in spite of my attire.

The next day our weather turned chilly again and stayed that way until the baby arrived. However, every year just before my daughter's birthday, when we think winter will never end, the same phenomenon occurs and everyone goes hunting for summer clothing once again. We've named this unique spring festivity Orange Popsicle Day and continue to celebrate it. Even our grandchildren have joined in. When that perfect day arrives (and it always does), we each enjoy an orange Popsicle wherever we are, or if possible, we meet somewhere to celebrate this refreshing custom together.

There is something magical about celebrating traditions. Children (and adults!) seem to flourish in an atmosphere where there are dependable customs to anticipate. Our niece says with delight, "Every Saturday morning, Dad makes pancakes." A friend tells me she and her husband have a standing date once a week. Our daughters love to recall the funny faces I drew with crayons on the hot shells of their soft-boiled breakfast eggs when they were young.

Perhaps traditions are reliable sources of comfort in a world that is uncertain. They provide a personal solace and sense of security and can also become a heritage for our families, passed on for generations. A tradition has the ability to turn a common day into an uncommon adventure. Give yourself and those you love the innocent pleasure of time-honored traditions.

BREAK FROM TRADITION

*Traditions…made up of
inherited passions and loyalties…*

EDITH WHARTON

little girl noticed that her mother always cut the ends from the ham before placing it in the roasting pan. When she asked why, her mother explained that her own mother had always done it. So the child asked her grandmother, who said she was simply following her mother's example. Finally, her great-grandmother solved the mystery when she admitted to cutting the ends off the ham because her old roasting pan was too small!

Although traditions provide a sense of comfort and security, it's also vital to recognize when it's time to leave certain customs behind. Sometimes we need to take a good look at how a tradition started, what purpose it served, and whether it's still effective. As life unfolds and experiences change, it's a good idea to stay flexible and open to new ideas.

This past Christmas holiday season, our growing family decided to depart from some well-established annual traditions. We chose to limit our gift-giving to a few meaningful items and instead spend our time and money on attending special events we could enjoy as a family. Our holiday plans focused first of all around celebrating the birth of Christ—the true reason for the season—and we attended musicals, dramas, and candlelight services at local churches. We also enjoyed carol singing, potluck suppers and board games with friends, live theater with the children, aromatherapy body massages for me and my daughters, and a day of tobogganing plus a dinner show with the entire family. There wasn't one complaint about a shortage of gifts to be opened, and no one went over their head financially. We all felt we'd had the most stress-free holiday season ever. Although making the change was still a challenge, this innocent pleasure was a big step toward liberation for all of us!

How easy it is to fall into a rut, becoming attached to traditions that may eventually get in the way of our inner peace. When we feel compelled or obligated by some external demanding force, traditions no longer bring the comfort they once offered. Good intentions turn into binding patterns and unrealistic expectations. When plans don't work out as anticipated, we feel let down, frustrated, and disappointed as we try to cope with yearnings for security that may only be an illusion after all.

Perhaps it's time to let go of an attachment and depart from some time-honored, firmly entrenched custom or routine. Breaking from tradition allows for creating a brand-new one!

WATER FUN

The great man is he who does
not lose his child's heart.

MENCIUS (372–289 B.C.)

One rainy Sunday morning after spending the night at our house, our granddaughter Alexandra asked if she and I could play outside for a bit before going to church. The idea of romping in the rain intrigued me, although I doubt I would have suggested it myself. So the two of us ventured out into the rain, still in our nightgowns, with bare feet and umbrellas over our heads. It was one of those warm summer showers—the kind where the sunshine streams through openings in the clouds and the rain is gentle and sweet smelling. As we danced and twirled over the wet lawn, we laughed, got dizzy, and fell down. We picked ourselves up again. We lifted our faces to the sky. I can imagine how preposterous we may have looked to passersby. Yet I am so thankful I didn't pass up the opportunity, and so pleased that a little girl prompted me to have my morning shower outdoors!

Children (and even some grown-up children) know there's joy in playing with water. When my own children were small, they squealed with joy in the bathtub and didn't want the experience to end. Our grandsons seem happiest when they're wading in a pool, getting sprayed by the hose, playing with toys that squirt water, or splashing in puddles. Children are attracted to water and delight in its benefits.

So enjoy the pleasures of water. Have fun with the garden hose. Play tag with the lawn sprinkler. Sit on the beach and let the waves roll over you. Frolic in the rain, or walk under an umbrella with someone special. Wear rubber boots and splash in the puddles, or do it barefoot. Dancing in the rain that day is one of the sweetest innocent pleasures I have stored in my memory, ready for me to draw on any time I choose.

PLAY TOURIST IN YOUR HOMETOWN

*Arise, walk through the land in
the length of it and in the breadth of it.*

GENESIS 13:17 KJV

Most of us dream of escaping the rat race for a while by packing up and going away. We assume we must drive for miles or hop on an airplane to get away from it all. In the meantime, others may be swarming to our area, traveling from faraway places to visit fascinating sites just around the corner from us. Why not seek out a few local tourist attractions and landmarks you take your guests to but would never think of visiting yourself?

On a recent island vacation, my husband and I paid the 75¢ fee to ride the local bus to the end of the line. Not only was it a great opportunity to do some people watching, but we got to see parts of the island that most residents admitted they don't visit. In fact, many of them were not able to give us details about some of the well-known tourist sites that we couldn't wait to see. Reading the brochures ahead of time gave us more particulars than some taxi drivers were able to provide.

The other day I abandoned my morning walking routine and instead drove to a nearby tourist town. What fun I had exploring many old familiar sights, but this time from a tourist's perspective. I took my camera and captured some unusual shots of popular sites, relaxed at an outdoor cafe with a cup of cappuccino, chatted with other visitors (the real tourists!), and toured a few galleries that featured local artists. What an enlightening and unforgettable experience!

Why not ride your local bus, ferry, or trolley to the end of the line, or spend an evening attending a professional sports game in your area? Visit historical museums or forts that detail the history of your region. Choose a nearby town or city, gather some tourist brochures, and plan your outing. Get up early one morning and spend the day exploring, either alone or with a friend. Whether you're roaming quaint boutiques, exploring exhibit halls, riding an antique train, or having lunch on the screened patio of a country inn, enjoying a bit of local culture may change the way you feel about your town and provide a unique getaway experience.

PLAY FOR FREE

There must be more to life than having everything.

MAURICE SENDAK

Do you ever feel like you can't afford to experience life to the fullest? For a jolt of creative fun, seek out the free or nearly free activities in your hometown. Most cities offer a variety of recreation and entertainment events that are open to the public at no charge, or at least at very affordable rates. It's simply a matter of ferreting them out. Once you've discovered what's available, make your personal list of favorites, and pick one now and then whenever you're in need of an affordable boost or can't remember when you enjoyed an outing that didn't cost an arm and a leg.

Take your favorite convertible or sports car for a test-drive, for example. You don't have to buy it, although you just may add it to your dream list once you've driven it. Art exhibits in the park are popular, as are summertime concerts, where you can hear anything from pop to jazz to gospel. It's a nice place to take a picnic, and you may be able to interview the musicians afterward. Volunteer as an usher at a theater, and you can see shows at no cost. Most performances, from student productions to professional musicals or operas, need ushers. Call the box office to find out how to participate. If there's a TV station near you, arrange to be in the studio audience. Producers are always on the lookout for lively spectators.

Seek out lunchtime seminars on a variety of topics, from financial planning to crafts, decorating, landscaping, and cooking. Often public lectures, workshops, and forums are advertised in local newspapers, church bulletins, and association newsletters. Many libraries also offer regular lectures and film series. In addition to circulating videos (for your own film festival?), books, games, and puzzles, today's libraries offer an array of services, including story and craft hours, summer reading clubs, and special after-school programs for kids. The popular super-bookstore chains host authors and musicians for readings and personal performances. This can be a fun and informative evening out with friends and a chance to meet your favorite author or performer in person!

Whether you're attending an ice cream social or local church spaghetti dinner, browsing through a fresh-air farmers' market, strolling through an old cemetery, visiting a museum, taking a garden tour of local homes, or watching planes take off and land at the airport, compare the feeling you have to a time when you spent a lot of money to be entertained. Playing for free just may be your choice in the future!

HAVE A FUN AND GAMES NIGHT

*The streets of the city will be filled
with boys and girls playing.*

ZECHARIAH 8:5 NASB

*F*riends and family know that when they are invited to our home, the board games are sure to appear, and an evening of laughter is in store. This game-playing penchant must run in the family because our grandsons now tell us one of their favorite family treats is games night. One evening a week, each child gets to choose his favorite game. Then a basket of hot buttered popcorn is passed around, and the fun begins. They play as many games as time will allow, choosing from board games old and new, charades, boisterous word games, and familiar card favorites like Crazy Eights or Old Maid. Crossword puzzles and brainteasers can be part of a games night as well. Try making up your own games. Or why not assemble a jigsaw puzzle, leaving it out on the table so family members and guests alike can add to it?

The lighthearted competition has a way of causing individual personality traits to emerge that might not be revealed any other time. Some folk are convinced that winning is sheer luck, while others believe that skill is the main factor. Either way, playing games is a great way to get to know others (and yourself) on a new level. Any wariness about participating and making a fool of oneself quickly dissipates in the friendly but serious sparring.

Even the less enthusiastic gamers often enjoy being part of a like-minded team. With a large group, participants can be divided into teams that rotate through several rooms. Teams can keep score at each station and then total all points at the end of the evening. Winning team members may receive an inexpensive prize or a homemade treat—or have everyone bring a "white elephant" prize along.

Get creative in planning your games night. Use old playing cards as coasters for glasses or for invitations, with the printed information glued to the decorative side. On a white paper tablecloth, use crayons to draw tic-tac-toe games for guests to play while waiting for snacks to be served. Make a simple centerpiece by gluing together a house of playing cards or scattering game markers and dice around a vase of flowers. Toss chocolate coins wrapped in gold foil on the table for decoration and nibbling.

When there's only two of you, don't forget about the old reliables: checkers, backgammon, and cribbage. If you haven't been seeing each other as much as you'd like, institute your own games night!

HAVE A
WINTER PICNIC

*Nature, in winter, provides the
greatest show on earth!*

f you're like most people who live in areas where they must brave the frigid, frosty climate of winter, it might not occur to you to have a picnic in the snow. Well, why not try it? For one thing, there are fewer people competing for picnic tables. There are no bugs, and you'll see some spectacular scenery that you'd miss if you were hunkering down by the fireplace, hibernating till spring arrives.

One winter picnic that our children still love to talk about took place in a wooded lot where my husband frequently chopped firewood. Bundled in warm, snugly snowsuits, woolen hats, and mittens, with knitted scarves wrapped tightly round our rosy faces, we made our way down the snowy path, hauling our sleigh behind. It was laden with jugs of hot cocoa, a basket chock-full of goodies, and our ice skates. Close to the clearing we chose was a tree-lined stream that had frozen over, making it the perfect sheltered spot for an afternoon of skating. After warming ourselves around a blazing bonfire, we roasted hot dogs to accompany our canteen of steaming soup, finishing off the meal with golden toasted marshmallows. Then it was time for skating. The children giggled and screamed as they learned to skate all over again on a surface that was less smooth than the flawless arena ice they were used to. When we'd had enough, we warmed up once again by the roaring fire and then went off to romp in the snow. We built a fort, created a giant snow family, and left behind lots of beautiful snow angels for the benefit of any resident deer or raccoons. We gathered up the other remnants of our stay and followed the familiar rule for any wilderness outing: "Take only pictures, leave only footprints."

Once we were back home, it was fun to curl up by the fireplace, sip mugs of hot cider, and wrap up in cozy quilts while we relived the day together. With the photographs we took, we can go back to that enchanting outing and reminisce any time we choose.

If you truly cannot get outdoors to enjoy your picnic, try having one inside. Spread a wool plaid blanket in the living room near a window. Roast hot dogs and toast marshmallows in the fireplace. Add some steamy hot chocolate topped with cinnamon, and play a few board games. Whether indoors or out, experience the wonders of a frosty winter day. Have a picnic. Make a memory.

PLAN A TREASURE HUNT

There comes a time in every rightly
constructed boy's life when he has
a raging desire to go somewhere
and dig for hidden treasure.

MARK TWAIN

You're never too old for a treasure hunt. Sometimes when I'm headed out of town, I leave a set of clues behind for my husband. After all, I wouldn't want him feeling too lonesome when I'm gone! I'll tuck the first under the bowl that holds his car keys so he'll be sure not to miss it. That clue might take him to the cupboard where I've left a small dish of nuts or his favorite cookies. The rest of the clues lead him all over the house until he finds the surprise I've left for him—perhaps a movie I know he wanted to watch, a new magazine that just came in the mail, or the pint of his favorite ice cream I hid in the freezer.

Treasure hunts have a long history in our household. We introduced our children to them at birthday parties, but they thought literally any occasion worthy of a trail of clues. Announce to Dad as he comes home from work that you're going on a picnic as soon as he finds the hidden basket. Or, for games night, let each child choose one to play. Wrap up the games (the newspaper comics are free and fun), hide them

181

around the house, and play them in the order the children find them.

One family extends the fun of Christmas morning with a treasure hunt. The tradition started the year their son received a tyke-sized basketball hoop. The first clue sat atop his stocking. The rest led him to the basement so he could try his first shots right away—playing basketball in the living room was not an option! As their children enter their teen years, they've made it clear that this tradition will continue.

Are your children too young to read clues? Draw pictures. Or hide enough things so they're sure to have success. At Easter time, don't bother filling plastic eggs with candy; little ones will relish the hunt itself, begging you to hide them again and again. Does someone claim they're too old for this? Turn the clues into cryptograms or conspire with your mate to think of an amazingly tough spot. Who would think of looking for their present inside the sleeve of a winter coat? Or a game in the fruit drawer of the refrigerator?

If you make this a tradition, the day will come when someone will surprise you with the first clue of a treasure hunt of your own. Happy hunting!

START A
COLLECTION

*Through knowledge its rooms are filled
with rare and beautiful treasures.*

PROVERBS 24:4 NIV

From the ridiculous to the sublime, from souvenir keepsakes to heirlooms, seeking out special treasures for personal collections can provide countless hours of fun. Few innocent pleasures compare to finding and displaying something you love. Beyond teddy bears, priceless figurines, classic cars, and Disney memorabilia, people collect everything from antique shoe buckles and ornate doorknobs to unique lunch boxes. My husband collects racing magazines and T-shirts with logos. My grandmother collected salt and pepper shakers, and a good friend collects ceramic rabbits.

And you'll simplify gift-buying dilemmas for others. What could be better, or easier, than picking up an addition to someone's favorite collection? When my husband shops for me, he is quite relieved that I collect teapots and not Corvettes!

While on vacation, adding to a collection is more fun than shopping for the traditional souvenirs that have a way of ending up in the back of the cupboard. There's an unmistakable thrill that comes with browsing in little, out-of-the-way shops, flea markets, or lawn sales and discovering the very object you were hunting for.

Don't overlook the collections you could start for free. Start filling a knickknack shelf with an unusual rock or shell from each beach you visit. Create an album filled with postcards or visitor's brochures from each historic site you explore.

Our various displays act as conversation starters. Guests often ask me to tell them where or how I acquired a certain item. Besides fascinating listening ears, the stories give me a chance to relive the circumstances that surrounded attaining a particular piece. The stories themselves become innocent pleasures and cherished memories.

Whether you collect to bring back the joys of childhood, for nostalgia, or for sheer aesthetic pleasure, accumulating and arranging prized possessions is pleasurable. My grandfather once confessed that when his job, family, or finances seemed out of control, he found peace in knowing his hundreds of *Reader's Digest* and *National Geographic* magazines were all in order!

ENJOY YOUR COLLECTION

What the heart has once owned
and had, it shall never lose.

HENRY WARD BEECHER

f you have a cherished collection, have you displayed it? Are the favorite things you've accumulated over the years visible? I have always been drawn to the ceremonial allure of serving afternoon tea, and so starting a collection of teapots seemed a natural thing to do. Now dozens of them are randomly clustered on shelves here and there and perched in rows atop kitchen cupboards. They are an enduring source of visual charm and entertainment. As I catch a glimpse of them adorning my sunlit kitchen, I stop and muse for a few moments, enjoy their unique patterns, and reflect on their distinguishing origins.

They range in appearance from pretty to preposterous, from princely to pleasing. Some are regal and elaborate with graceful appeal, while others are delightfully whimsical. A few are even eccentric or wildly ludicrous, but all are interesting and have their own particular heritage. I found one of my favorites in a hotel gift shop while I was on a business trip—a fanciful dancing girl with a generous bosom and an enormous ruffled petticoat in shocking pink. She's doing the can-can; one of her legs kicked high forms the spout.

According to the season or special events taking place in our home, I choose one or two teapots as decorative accessories. The beautiful bunny rabbit, a Mother's Day gift from my daughters, decked out in her finest fashions including a flamboyant Easter bonnet, takes center stage each spring along with the "head of lettuce" teapot and "tomato" cream pitcher and sugar bowl—pieces of another collection! Each winter, out comes the quaint storybook cottage donned with a snow-covered rooftop and looking almost angelic with candlelit windows and pretty wreaths. I purchased it during a speaking tour in England.

Some are simply decorative; others are practical and functional. The elegant Queen Victoria, inherited from my grandmother, comes to life at a breezy summer afternoon chat with friends on the porch, complete with lace tablecloth, linen napkins, tiny sandwiches, and fancy cakes. The blue and white piano with the kitten sleeping on top, a birthday gift from two dear friends, is perfect when I celebrate teatime on Saturday morning with our granddaughters.

Relish your collections. Bring them out into the open where you can appreciate them. Think of ways to create interesting and engaging displays. These tangible remembrances are to be enjoyed. Once in a while, take some time to delight in each piece, an innocent pleasure that allows you to travel back in time, savoring sweet memories along the way.

MEMORY GIFTS

*The foreground of life
depends on the background.*

One year for Christmas, my mother assembled five scrapbooks, one for each of her children. She searched through hoards of snapshots in order to select just the right ones. In every album she arranged pictures of each child along with corresponding memorabilia such as certificates, newspaper clippings, ticket stubs to special events, and other mementos. She personalized the pages with handwritten details and short anecdotes relating to various events. What a touching experience it was to look at it for the first time. I love knowing I can sit and browse through my life story anytime I choose! My sisters all agree that these gifts of love are precious tangible reminders of how we spent our early years, keeping memories alive of the meaningful events and people from our past.

Recently I was asked to contribute to a memory gift for some good friends who were celebrating a special wedding anniversary out of town. Their children wrote to dozens of friends from across the country who couldn't attend the celebration, asking that we mail photos of ourselves (preferably taken with the couple being honored). They also suggested we include a written recollection, a favorite memory, or some special thought about them and their marriage that would let them know how much we appreciate them. The family is planning to assemble the photos and comments in an album to be presented at the party. I'm sure it's going to be treasured by this couple forever.

Your memory gift doesn't have to be a completed project. One year I gave each of my grandchildren an album partially filled with photos I had taken of them over the summer holidays. Now at the end of each summer, I give them new summertime snapshots to add. You may want to start someone off with a good-quality album or scrapbook, along with a few photos that you've taken yourself or gathered from their own collection that follow a certain theme. What an innocent pleasure it is to give a gift that keeps on giving over the years!

PUT YOUR MEMORIES ON DISPLAY

*Memories are the essence of our
personal identity and all we truly own.*

*D*oes the sight of an ornate photo album overwhelm you with guilt over the hoards of photos crammed away in drawers and boxes or plastered on bulletin boards and fridge doors when they should be dated and properly mounted in albums? For some of us, it's a challenge merely to take pictures and get them developed! Yet whether stuffed in a shoe box, labeled in scrapbooks, or displayed in picture frames, our photographs are steadfast reminders and permanent records of our life events. We have a summary of the cherished memories—visual artifacts of people, places, pets, and events—that we don't want to forget. When we browse through them with the sole purpose of enjoying them, photos turn the past into something tangible we can hold, look at, and return to any time we desire.

Discovering unique ways to display old photographs can be a rewarding and worthwhile pastime. Find a picture of yourself when you were six, put it in a whimsical frame, and place it where you can see it daily to reawaken the child in you. Create groupings of several photos to hang in a hallway or quiet nook, or arrange them on a desk or tabletop. Place a few albums out in the open handy for browsing, and alternate them according to the occasion. Find a sturdy box with a lid and, using decoupage, cover it completely with a composition of cropped photographs. These make great storage boxes. Kids will have loads of fun making their own.

Here's a space-saving idea: Take some pictures of the children with their school or science projects, especially the extra bulky ones, so you can keep the photo and dispose of the project—without guilt! For flexible display areas, use a framed corkboard and change your memories often. Or have a piece of glass cut to fit your desktop and slip favorite snapshots along with quotes and other memorabilia underneath. Their images will peek out from under your work all day to comfort and encourage you.

As you recall people and places of your past from a new standpoint and with fresh insights and a more mature outlook, you may see things you missed before. And with your photos visible, you'll be more apt to take a stroll down memory lane with family and friends, recalling old times and sharing anecdotes to go with them. Who knows, you may learn some interesting *new* stories, too!

A PHOTO MEMOIR STORYBOOK

*Photography is an art form which
isolates single moments for all time.*

One of the few legacies you have to pass on (and one of the first possessions I, for one, would save from a burning house) is that box full of photographs tucked away somewhere. Those photos can become an ongoing celebration of your life and will be easier to pass down to future generations once you get them sorted and arranged. Organizing your pictures has probably been on your To Do list for ages, but now, with the increasing popularity of making scrapbooks, there are books and classes to show you novel and practical ways to preserve your photo memories. It's actually possible to get it done and have fun at the same time.

Start by digging out your shoe-box collection of snapshots, and pick a spot where you can leave your temporary project undisturbed. Lay out your supplies: ring-style binder albums, acid-free paper in a variety of colors, scissors, a ruler, decorative shapes, caption stickers, photo corners or double-sided tape for mounting, and pigment ink pens or pencils for labeling. Use brightly colored pens, decorative materials, or caption stickers to enhance the photos and help tell the story. It's fun to add black-and-white photos, which could also be hand-tinted using tinting oils available in many art supply shops. Crop some photos by cutting away blank spaces or distracting images, and you'll strengthen your photograph by focusing attention on the subject of the picture.

Instead of attempting to tackle the entire project in one sitting, take a few spare moments here and there to return to it, sorting and savoring your collection a bit at a time. Consider working on your project with others—it's a great opportunity to spend time with family members or friends. Arranging and displaying photographs is not only fun but also relaxing and therapeutic. Reminiscing with photos of your life events creates a sense of belonging. It affirms to the children in our lives that they are a significant part of our world. Photos give a great sense of family identity and provide a means of preserving treasured memories, not only for our own enjoyment but to also pass down from generation to generation.

PHOTO
STORYBOOK
THEMES

*For a crowd is not company; and faces are
but a gallery of pictures; and talk but
a tinkling cymbal, where there is no love.*

FRANCIS BACON

Instead of the typical chronological photo album, choose topics for your memoir albums ahead of time. A subject or theme can chronicle an event that lasts a day, such as a party or holiday gathering, or perhaps annual events—dance recitals, sporting seasons, or Halloween costumes. Here are a few ideas to spark your creativity:

- a family reunion, with some shots capturing several generations

- holiday celebrations such as the Fourth of July or Thanksgiving

- baby's first bath, first visit to grandma's, first step, first tooth, first haircut, etc.

- a retirement party, school reunion, or milestone birthday

- a single vacation or a collection of scenic photos from all your travels

- beautiful sunsets or unusual signs you've spotted over time

- a day spent at the beach, at the playground, or splashing in the rain

- the progression of your new home construction, renovations, or landscaping

- family pets

- kids—bath time, school events, cookie baking, fishing trips, kite flying, swimming

- lazy days of summer or a winter ski trip

- any family gathering or group outing

Working with your theme is a good way to prevent "photo build-up" by getting rid of unflattering, boring, or repetitious shots. Give doubles away to those who will appreciate them. Toss out all the rest or save a few to make collages of special people or occasions. Free yourself from holding on to every one, and it will be easier to make this innocent pleasure a regular practice.

PART 8

TEA FOR TWO...OR MORE!

DEEPEN THE BONDS OF FRIENDSHIP

A friend is a present you give yourself.

ROBERT LOUIS STEVENSON

There are many ways to describe a genuine friend: a person with shared experiences or the same sense of humor, someone who wants to be with you in the same way you want to be with him, one you can be silent with, someone who *doesn't* buy your child a drum or a horn as a birthday present! Friends love you unconditionally and are as committed to your joy, prosperity, and inner peace as you are to theirs.

A friend is someone who stimulates and awakens in you thoughts, ideals, and creativity you never knew were there, causing you to stretch to reach your full capacity. A true friend is someone who will laugh and cry with you because both tears of joy and sadness can create a bond like nothing else. Most of all, I believe the best friend is one who knows all about you and loves you anyway. A friend always gives you a second chance when the rest of the world gives up on you. As Samuel Johnson put it, "You can always tell a real friend: When you've made a fool of yourself, he doesn't feel you've done a permanent job!" Friendship needs to be a safe refuge where you can think aloud, express your ideas, and dare to be yourself without the fear of rejection. In true friendship, you never have to play games or pretend you're someone you're not.

I have just come from a get-together with a small group of friends where we worked on some crafts to be used at an upcoming community event. For three hours, as we worked and enjoyed coffee and muffins, we laughed even while tears streamed down our faces, and we shared our dreams, hopes, needs, and concerns. In short, we shared our hearts. I am convinced that it's in those intimate chats, if we listen closely, that we will hear the voice of God revealing heavenly wisdom to us.

My friends and I talked about the need to be together more often. So many of us secretly yearn for the innocent pleasure of deeper, richer, more meaningful relationships. Friends, like flowers in the garden of life, truly are presents you give yourself.

NURTURE YOUR
FRIENDSHIPS

I didn't find my friends;
the good God gave them to me.

RALPH WALDO EMERSON

There's a proverb that says, "Old shoes and old friends are best." Friends are our best buffers in times of stress, our best supporters in times of loneliness, and our best encouragers in times of change. Yet do we spend time consciously developing a well-thought-out plan for reinforcing those relationships? We may appreciate our good friends and the role they play in our lives, but if we believe great friendships merely happen, we may not invest the time and effort required to sustain them.

Life-nourishing relationships are easily eroded by our frenzied, time-pressured lifestyles. Therefore, we need a good supply of innocent pleasures that will tenderly care for our friendships and strengthen the bonds we hold dear. How about something as simple as taking your morning or evening walk with a friend or starting a book club? One group of friends I know will read the same book and then meet over afternoon tea to share what they gleaned from it. Another group has invited me to be part of a "girls' day out" while our husbands race cars together at a special yearly event. With a little planning and effort, our friendships can be enriched. Revere your friends. Build and nurture your relationships, and they will add pleasure to your life.

Consider the law of reciprocity. Friendship is a two-way street. As Max Mandelstamm suggests, "Friendship is a treasury, and you cannot take from it more than you put into it." Both give and both take. Otherwise, one is bound to feel taken advantage of or imposed upon.

We all need someone in our life who believes in us; who supports our dreams, goals, and plans; who encourages us, cheering us on, reassuring us we have what it takes to get through life's obstacle course. Let your friends know often how much you value them and the gift of their friendship. Then your true friends will be here today *and* here tomorrow!

I went out to find a friend but could not find one there;
I went out to be a friend, and friends were everywhere!

AUTHOR UNKNOWN

HOSPITALITY PLEASURES

Without fellowship,
life is not worth living.

LAURIE COLWIN

s with so many other innocent pleasures in our lives—assembling our photographs, sending a handwritten note, starting a family tradition— many of us procrastinate when it comes to hospitality. Too often, we make entertaining into such a big event that we feel overwhelmed at the mere thought of it. We invest more time, money, and effort when company's coming than we normally would for ourselves. In our planning, shopping, cooking, and attempts to create the ideal atmosphere, our regular routines (and finances!) can be disrupted for days or even weeks.

Last summer, I invited a couple we know to join my husband and me for lunch on the patio. The plan was to toss a few wieners on the barbecue and open a bag of potato chips. Then, not wanting some other mutual friends to feel left out, we invited them, too. Since I was investing the time and effort anyway, it made sense to invite a few more, and soon we had 24 people coming. Hot dogs were replaced with steaks, the chips became potato salad, ice-cream cones turned into homemade cakes and pies, and soft drinks in cans were now pitchers of lemonade and iced tea. Before I knew it, I was out of control. The patio furniture didn't look that hot, so I replaced it with some new pieces. The spare bathroom suddenly needed to be painted and wallpapered, which also meant buying new accessories. Yes, I was exhausted and broke by the time our guests arrived. I greeted them at the door feeling as though I never wanted to entertain again.

Why do we do it to ourselves? When our children were young and we didn't have the funds or time to fuss like that, my dinner parties were served in the kitchen and consisted of one-course meals and simple desserts. Often, part of the fun was getting everybody involved in the preparation. Evening entertainment included a few games, a bowl of popcorn, and a late-night snack of peanut butter cookies and a basket of apples. Each week, someone else took a turn in their home. It was loads of fun and not much work for anyone. After my extravagant and costly luncheon escapade, I'm convinced that simple entertaining is an innocent pleasure worth reviving!

TEA FOR TWO... OR MORE!

Come oh come ye tea-thirsty restless ones—
the kettle boils, bubbles and sings musically.

RABINDRANATH TAGORE

From the time our granddaughter could hold a cup, the two of us have been enjoying tea parties. We visit one of the Victorian tearooms in the quaint nearby tourist town of Niagara-on-the-Lake, dressed in our floral frocks and adorned with jewelry and flamboyant hats. Now it's fun to see her host pretend tea parties with her dolls and teddy bears and sometimes even the cat as she serves animal crackers and pours invisible tea into tiny toy cups.

On occasion, we invite her boy cousins to join us. It's quite amazing to see them switch into their "polite and refined" mode once they sit down to an attractively set tea table. Tea parties and the act of pretending to be a grown-up offer children a magical way of learning table manners.

Sometimes we hire "Tea Granny," a captivating local story-teller and innovative businesswoman who serves tea picnics in the park for children's parties. She brings along old trunks full of elaborate costumes and exquisite accessories, and the children giggle with delight as they play dress-up in front of a mirror propped up against an old tree trunk. Of course, the tea is very weak; most of the fun comes from adding milk and stirring. Or fruit juice is substituted—poured from a pot, just like tea. Cucumber sandwiches are replaced with peanut butter and banana, or cream cheese blended with marmalade, but the ritual is the same. Children love ceremony, and I'm convinced we do, too.

Occasionally, I visit a charming tearoom with a group of friends where the hostess, "Lady Victoria," greets us dressed in an old-fashioned lace wedding gown complete with bustle, elaborate hat, and long silk gloves. We stop in her hat room to choose just the right one to complement our outfits. The charming collection of mismatched teacups, delicate china plates, shining silver tied together with ribbons in soft colors, and immaculate starched linen make it a delightful experience. Add delicious finger sandwiches garnished with parsley sprigs, fancy iced cakes, scones with strawberries and cream, and special friends to share the pleasure, and the afternoon becomes a welcome retreat.

A tea party is a refreshing change from other types of mealtime entertaining. There is a closeness and affection we experience sipping tea with others. Dreams are born and memories shared. And, as Catherine Douzel reminds us, "Each cup of tea represents an imaginary voyage."

MEALS WITH FRIENDS

So they ate and were well filled.

PSALM 78:29

To me, food tastes better when it's shared. We all have to eat dinner somewhere, so we may as well have a meal together now and then. But there is a problem. Even thought we crave the fellowship, the planning, shopping, preparing, and cooking for others at the end of a long workday can be agonizing. At one time, I wouldn't dream of inviting company for supper during the week—it was just too much work. Then I decided there must be ways we could gather our friends together at the table to enjoy a simple, savory, no-fuss supper now and again. That's when I discovered several interesting types of dining that could become innocent pleasures.

Potluck suppers, for example, are enjoying a resurgence today and help to keep entertaining simple. Each family taking part provides a single dish, and the meal quickly evolves into a delicious, full-fledged banquet. After all, when people are invited to dinner, they often ask what they can bring along anyway and are happy to contribute. With as few as three individuals, couples, or families, it's possible to serve a balanced meal with one providing the main dish, another the salad, and the third a dessert. You may want to make it a rule that only plates, cups, and napkins that can be recycled or disposed of are to be used, especially when time and energy are limited. Encourage guests to bring copies of their recipes to hand out, because someone will nearly always ask for them. You may even start your group's personalized recipe book!

On occasion we invite a new neighbor, someone at work or church we've been wanting to get to know better, or a single person who may not always be invited to an event with couples or families. We started doing this monthly with a small group of friends. Now many of our guests duplicate these "fellowship suppers" in their own homes.

Progressive dinners are fun, too! Have guests start out in one home for an appetizer, then move to the next for the main course, reaching their final destination for dessert and coffee. Some friends we know choose to do this in a series of restaurants instead of homes, and although the cost may be higher, there's literally no work for anyone. The underlying foundation of entertaining as an innocent pleasure is to remember the k.i.s.s. formula: keep it sweet and simple!

SPONTANEOUS ENTERTAINING

The cheerful heart has
a continual feast.

Proverbs 15:15 niv

n my thesaurus, some other words for spontaneous are *impulsive, unconstrained, casual,* and *free.* Doesn't that sound like a terrific way to entertain? Getting together with people you enjoy doesn't have to be costly or involved. For most of us, what we truly crave when we have company, even more than the food or entertainment, is the fun, camaraderie, and intimate conversation. Spontaneity lets you get together with others more often.

Don't panic. This really isn't as hard as it sounds. Think about some of those spur-of-the-moment activities in the past that just "happened." Chances are you even commented on how enjoyable spontaneous events are because they're so simple. Expectations are basically nonexistent, and anything goes because it wouldn't be conceivable to achieve the perfect setting and ideal meal! So why not *plan* to have more impromptu events?

Pick up the phone. Some of our favorite memories are of times we called friends at the last minute to be our guests at a neighborhood church supper, spaghetti dinner, or fish fry we saw advertised on a poster in town. Or pack your meal in a picnic basket, call a few friends to suggest they do the same, and meet them at a nearby park or beach. You could ask everyone back to your home for dessert and coffee—stop by the store for ice cream on the way.

Don't put it off any longer! Yes, you could wait until the living room carpet has been replaced or you finally get those new dishes, but there will always be too much to do and the time will never be right. We liberated ourselves from this mindset the night we decided to have a dinner party even though we were right in the middle of major renovations to our home. With piles of lumber and workmen's tools all around us, we laughed the evening away, and even our guests said they felt as though they had been set free. The next time you're tempted to postpone entertaining until all conditions are perfect, remind yourself it's the conversation and companionship you're looking for. The important thing is to keep *planning* spontaneity until it becomes a simple and natural innocent pleasure.

CREATIVE MEALS

Feasts are made for laughter.

<small>ECCLESIASTES 10:19 NRSV</small>

With a little imagination, you can turn a simple meal into a fun-filled event that will leave you with many special memories. One idea is to create a theme based on the season, your nationality, or the culture and customs of your guests. Our wonderful Italian friends occasionally invite us for an informal family-style spaghetti dinner with huge meatballs, warm crusty bread, and a big tossed salad. They added atmosphere with red candles in canning-jar holders filled with dry macaroni, and they served the meal on red checkered tablecloths with matching napkins. Manicotti could be used for napkin rings and bucatini—a long, thin, hollow pasta—for drinking straws.

Try a Hawaiian luau with glazed chicken wings, rice salad, coconut cream pie, and pineapple punch, or an Oriental supper of sweet and sour meatballs, fried rice, and fortune cookies. What about a New England clam bake with Boston baked beans, roasted corn on the cob, brown bread, and hot apple cider? A Mexican meal might include tortillas, a taco salad, and some chilled lemonade. My husband is of Polish decent and enjoys offering guests a traditional feast of pierogi, cabbage rolls, and sauerkraut with sausage. Naturally, we play polka music in the background, and guests dance in their seats through the entire meal!

For a fun theme, have breakfast alfresco. It's enjoyable to eat any meal outdoors, but breakfast on the patio is a special treat. It's not that common and can be kept fairly simple. Serve anything from barbecued back bacon, grilled tomatoes, and scrambled eggs cooked in a cast iron skillet to a watermelon basket brimming with fresh fruit, ham and cheese quiche, and banana-walnut pancakes topped with warm maple syrup. Add a few pitchers of fruit juice, a pot of freshly brewed coffee, and some bakery muffins, coffee cake, or nut loaves—we have guests bring their favorites—and you've got an event that may become the highlight of your summer.

Occasionally, try an open house. It's a refreshing change from the usual parties, and since people are coming and going, it offers a chance to see more friends on one occasion. Make dishes ahead and keep serving simple by choosing finger foods that can be eaten at room temperature. Whether it's a "homemade personal pizza" party or "make-your-own ice cream sundaes," theme parties are innocent pleasures that turn any meal into an event!

SEND THANK-YOU NOTES

Kind hearts are the garden,
kind thoughts are the roots.
Kind words are the blossoms,
kind deeds are the fruits.

JOHN RUSKIN

We all have many people we can be thankful for, including family, friends, neighbors, coworkers, and people from our past who contributed to our lives in one way or another. Take a few moments once a week to think of someone you could thank, and then let them know in writing how much you appreciate them. Consider the special teacher or a particular boss who encouraged you by seeing some attribute or strength you would never have recognized in yourself. Think of the neighbor who keeps a watchful eye on your home when you're away or the courier who gets your deliveries to you on time. Write a letter to your spouse's parents, telling them how much you love their child. Near your anniversary, send a note to your original wedding party, thanking them once again for their part in your happiness. You may even want to write a love note to God, expressing heartfelt words of devotion and appreciation. Telling the heavenly Father we love Him also reminds us of His incredible love for us.

Although it seems extremely simplistic, this innocent pleasure may be a life-changing habit. Sending a note of thanks seems to be one innocent pleasure that's become a lost art. We all like to be acknowledged and appreciated, yet most of us neglect to make the effort to let others know they are valued. In some cases, it's just a matter of politeness. My mother (and Miss Manners) drilled that into me while I was growing up. If you've ever sent a gift and never heard whether it was received, you know the significance of sending even a short note of gratitude.

My husband and I recently organized a small dinner party with a group of old friends with whom we had lost contact. It was fun to reconnect, and when I received a beautiful note from one of the guests thanking us for a memorable evening, I couldn't resist calling to say thanks for the thank-you! Although it seemed a funny thing to do, being thanked in writing is so rare that I just had to let her know I treasured her thoughtfulness.

Try sending a thank-you note to someone you had as a guest in your home. Think of what a delightful surprise it will be! If you truly enjoyed their company, it's okay to let them know. Make it easy to say thanks by keeping a supply of attractive stationery and assorted notes on hand. Set up a writing center complete with stamps, a good pen, some envelopes, and a list of favorite quotes. Then, when the mood strikes, you'll be all set to let someone know how special they are!

PHONE A FRIEND

*What do we live for, if it is not
to make life less difficult for each other?*

GEORGE ELIOT

y daughters, who both lead full lives as moms, homemakers, and college students, shared with me recently that they have discovered an innocent pleasure of their own. It's a unique way to make life less difficult for each other by taking some of the drudgery out of their daily chores. They plan a time that they can call and chat on their cordless phones while getting some routine tasks out of the way. Whether unloading the dishwasher, folding and distributing clean laundry, packing lunches, tidying up, organizing a drawer, or going from room to room gathering stray items, there are many tasks they can accomplish while having a good visit on the phone. Although I've always felt it's better not to be tackling chores that are distracting while talking on the phone, when the call is planned ahead of time with an understanding between both parties, it can be a pleasurable way to check off a few more items on the perpetual To Do list!

Lately, I've tapped into their idea and use it as a way to stay in touch with special people in my life when I must put off getting together in person. Now and then, I'll arrange to simply have a morning coffee break over the phone with a good friend. Sometimes I'll have lunch with one of my sisters or a late-night toast-and-tea with my mother. Let's face it— there are times when meeting in person isn't possible because of time or distance.

While I'd rather visit with my family or friends face-to-face, it doesn't always work out. And visits on the phone sure beat the alternative of not being in touch at all. Is there a friend or family member you've been longing to visit? If you just can't seem to arrange a meeting in person to catch up, why not phone a friend to enjoy morning coffee, afternoon tea, or lunch together, and maybe even catch up on some chores at the same time.

SHARE THE LAUGHTER

*Grief can take care of itself, but to get
the full value of joy, you must
have somebody to divide it with.*

MARK TWAIN

aughter is best when shared with another person.
The next time you watch a comical movie or a live
comedian, observe what happens during the really
hilarious parts—people automatically turn to look at the
person next to them, even if they are strangers and have had no
contact up to that point. They experience the humor together.
In my travels, I've seen it happen time and time again, whether
watching a movie in a theater or on an airplane, leading a fun
session in my seminars, and even worshiping in a church ser-
vice. It seems our enjoyment of laughter is multiplied when we
share it with someone else.

A friend claims that she and her brothers all inherited the
same sense of humor as well as the same nose! They each know
several Bill Cosby records and Marx Brothers movie scenes by
heart. As teenagers, doing the dishes meant quoting those lines
back and forth until someone got stuck. The loser had to finish
cleaning up the kitchen. Now, years later, their spouses aren't

sure whether to laugh or cry when a one-liner launches them into the old routines.

Make a point of spending time with people who make you laugh and also those who bring out your own funny side. Often it takes a special person to help develop our own unique sense of humor. Even if you don't see yourself a clown by nature, I'm convinced there's a comedian hidden inside most of us, longing to bring joy to the world. Besides, when laughter is shared, it has an amazing way of uniting us. Laughing truly creates a universal bond.

READ TO SOMEONE

Books are keys to wisdom's treasure;
books are gates to lands of pleasure;
Books are paths that upward lead;
books are friends, come let us read.

EMILE POULSSON

esterday I had lunch with a friend who told me that she and her husband have discovered the innocent pleasure of reading to each other in the evenings. Since they both love to read, they now take turns sharing their favorite books instead of each reading alone. Because their interests are different, they each benefit from a new perspective. And it's a pleasant and refreshing alternative to watching television "just for the sake of watching."

I get teased for always having too many books on the go at once. My husband readily admits that although he enjoys reading specific types of literature, he is far from being a bookworm. He does, however, enjoy having me read aloud to him. When I do, it provides just as much satisfaction for me.

Reading to someone fulfills the desire to share a well-told story. It is not about proclaiming one's personal ideals, beliefs, or moral codes. Rather, it stimulates the emotions of the human spirit and disseminates some truths of life. When I read to Cliff, our imaginations are inspired, our sense of humor is enlivened, and our awareness is raised. Fresh perspectives take root as we mutually contemplate new viewpoints. These are times when we laugh and cry together. The process becomes a shared experience, binding both reader and listener. Cliff has begun reading to me, and now we enjoy the reciprocal sharing of what is significant and meaningful to each of us. I cherish those moments; they have provided extraordinary insights into what matters most to each of us.

I also find the sound of his voice immensely comforting. Many of us have fond recollections of having been read to as children. The soothing sound of a parent's voice, the classic books, and the familiar stories all combine to provide a sense of certainty and assurance. We remember the stories we were told, because they are timeless and because someone special read them to us. Those times create vivid images in our minds for years to come. We know that a picture is worth a thousand words. If that is true, then a story read aloud is worth a million.

BE CREATIVE
IN GIFT GIVING!

The only gift is a portion of yourself.
The gift without the giver is bare.

JAMES RUSSELL LOWELL

gift can be anything you do for someone to show kindness, compassion, or understanding. I love to receive faxes from a friend who likes to send me gifts of inspiring quotes, funny riddles, humorous sayings, or simply messages that say "Hello—thinking of you!" Another friend calls some mornings with a proverb or Scripture verse from a daily devotional book that she believes may encourage me that day. Amazingly, the messages seem to arrive exactly when I need a boost, and they can alter the entire focus of my day. Someone else I know clips and saves magazine or newspaper articles I'll be interested in and uses them as an excuse to meet over coffee. I've picked up many of these ideas and am thrilled to pass them on to others when I see the opportunity.

Consider delivering flowers or a casserole to someone when it's most needed and least expected, or send an occasional note in the mail to offer comfort or to simply say "I appreciate you." When meeting someone for lunch, pick up a single rose or a bouquet from a street vendor on the way.

Plan an annual outing with friends that you can look forward to all year. Celebrate each other's birthdays by going out for lunch or dinner together instead of buying gifts. I am part of a group of friends who were born in the same year, one in each of the seasons. We meet for dinner on our birthdays, so we get to see each other at least four times a year.

Another friend came up with the idea of visiting restaurants alphabetically. It's fun to seek out enough local spots to fill in all the letters!

If a friend is sick, instead of sending the usual flowers, fill a get-well basket with small items appropriate for the bedside—hand cream, a crossword puzzle book, scented soap, a pretty notepad and pen, assorted fruit teas, a book on tape, magazines, a small book of quotes. Wrap them individually and label them the days of the week. Attach a note letting your friend know these are "one-a-day" presents. My mother did this for me once when I was bedridden, and I never forgot it!

When choosing gifts for friends, opt for something out of the ordinary, something they'd probably never buy themselves. Creativity in gift giving has less to do with what or how much you give than it does with giving something meaningful at just the right moment!

LOVE AND BE LOVED

Thou shalt love thy neighbour as thyself.

LEVITICUS 19:18

ntimate and loving moments shared with other people make life pleasurable. As you look back, you'll probably find that the moments when you have truly lived are those when you have done things in the spirit of love. All great teachers, masters, and spiritual leaders agree that giving love is the most valuable use of our time and energy, and that being loved is the most basic need in our lives. I don't know anyone who doesn't want a little more love in life. Victor Hugo told us, "Life's greatest happiness is to be convinced we are loved." How is it, then, that we have forgotten to love, or that we never learned to love in the first place?

You may have heard that love is something we keep by giving it away. The truth is you can't give love away or receive it until you love yourself. When you do, you'll nurture and care for yourself by staying fit and healthy, spending time in nature, praying and meditating, pampering yourself now and then, and taking time out to do what you enjoy. You become a wellspring of love rather than an empty vessel waiting for others to supply the love you need and desire. If you're trying to give love even though you are running on empty yourself, consider that looking after your own needs is *not* self-centered—you're not able to give away what you don't own. Before you can love others, you have to be filled up.

When you become a channel of love rather than a receptacle, you'll discover one of the most remarkable secrets of joy and contentment. The more love you give away, the more you'll receive! Today, truly open your heart and extend loving thoughts to others. Lavish love on every living thing—your family, friends, neighbors, coworkers, pets, and strangers. Practice sending out invisible rays of love wherever you go—in traffic, at a staff meeting, in the grocery store—and see how much better you feel at the end of the day. Notice how a bad situation improves and how other people's responses are more positive.

Every day, think of someone you can love. Tell at least one person something you like, admire, or appreciate about them. Get in the habit of saying "I love you," "I'm proud of you," and "I'm thankful for you" regularly. Start experiencing unconditional love by accepting yourself, others, and the amazing love of God. Love is like a little haven of refuge from the cares of the day. As St. Augustine wrote, "He who is filled with love is filled with God Himself."

CONCLUSION

*I*ndulging in innocent pleasures is a lifestyle. Choosing to add delight, comfort, and joy to each day doesn't stop when your life improves, when you get the ideal job, when your relationships are going well, and when all your problems seem to fade. It is an ongoing process.

Integrating innocent pleasures into your daily living brings change, energy, and renewal. You'll view the world differently and notice things you might otherwise have overlooked. Whether you do one a day or two a week, I encourage you to implement as many of the innocent pleasures presented here as you can. Discover your own and add to those in this book. When you do, I believe you'll be inspired to view your life and the world around you differently. My prayer is that you will be transformed, and your life will be incredibly enriched!

"Just living is not enough," said the butterfly. "One must have freedom, sunshine, and a little flower."

HANS CHRISTIAN ANDERSEN

*Other Great Harvest House Books
by Sue Augustine*

TURN YOUR DREAMS INTO REALITIES

Sue Augustine reveals powerful strategies, practical keys, and examples from her inspirational story that will motivate you to see your dreams through to reality and to embrace your passions, calling, and purpose.

WHEN YOUR PAST IS HURTING YOUR PRESENT

In this encouraging book, Sue Augustine presents a clear and manageable path to reconciling a painful past based on sound biblical principles, using her own heart-rending story to lead you to a future full of hope.

To learn more about books by Sue Augustine
or to read sample chapters, log on to our website:

www.harvesthousepublishers.com

HARVEST HOUSE PUBLISHERS
EUGENE, OREGON
